MW01057855

REMEDIES
IN A NUTSHELL
By

WILLIAM M. TABB
Professor and Judge Fred A. Daugherty Chair in Law
University of Oklahoma

ELAINE W. SHOBEN
Edward W. Cleary Professor of Law
University of Illinois

Mat #40140052

Nutshell Series, In a Nutshell, the Nutshell Logo and West Group are trademarks registered in the U.S. Patent and Trademark Office.

© 2005 Thomson/West
        610 Opperman Drive
        P.O. Box 64526
        St. Paul, MN 55164–0526
        1–800–328–9352

ISBN 0–314–14604–0

*To our loving and supportive spouses,
Diane Tabb and Ed Shoben*

*

PREFACE

This Nutshell on Remedies provides an overview of judicial remedies. It explores the substantive requirements for major remedies at law and in equity as well as the practical considerations that aid with context and application. The study of Remedies is challenging because it arises in all areas of law – statutory, constitutional, and common law. The questions of remedial availability and effectiveness are among the most important issues in law because the potential remedy in a case reflects the extent to which the right may be vindicated. One of the central themes in this book is the relationship between "rights" and "remedies" and how a right is only as great as the remedy that protects it.

In most law schools, Remedies is a capstone course that builds on the study of first year subjects in torts, property, contracts, and civil procedure. It assumes familiarity with the substantive doctrines that form the basis for establishing rights under those areas of law, such as whether negligence exists or a contract breach has occurred. The issue of remedies arises when one or more legally recognizable right exists and has been violated. The question then becomes determining what remedies may be available to enforce, vindicate, redress or compensate that right.

Other major themes in this book include the selection of the most effective remedy when alternative remedies may be available and the relationship of multiple remedies to each other. For example, the victim of embezzlement may seek either damages or restitution, but not both. In contrast, someone who has suffered an injury to land for repeated trespasses may have multiple and compatible remedies. In many cases involving injuries to land, the innocent landowner may seek compensatory damages for the harm suffered and may also seek equitable relief to prevent invasions in the future. The study of remedies includes the entitlement and measurement of damages, the principles guiding equitable relief, and the process by which law and equity may be applied for the benefit of the landowner in such a case.

The organization of the book reflects the four classifications of remedies: injunctions, damages, restitution and declaratory relief. The major remedial alternatives are examined within each classification. Therefore, the study of injunctions considers the various types of temporary orders, permanent injunctions, and specific performance. The study of compensatory damages for contract breach evaluates both the common law rules and those under Article II of the Uniform Commercial Code.

In order to gain more insight into the practical application of each area, the book also evaluates the important defenses, exceptions, limitations and adjustments to the basic remedies. Thus, the study of equity becomes more fully understood by evaluating the requirements of civil and criminal contempt to enforce equitable decrees. The examination of damages is completed by matters such as the doctrine of avoidable consequences and the rules of discounting to present value for lump sum awards in personal injury cases. The exploration of equitable restitution similarly includes the limiting doctrines of tracing, change of position, volunteers and the bona fide purchaser for value rule.

We have sought to provide a book that can provide a general survey of the subject for any reader. We have also tried to produce a useful accompaniment to any casebook for law students. The materials provide references to leading cases in each substantive area, Restatement provisions, or statutory citations in order to facilitate understanding and application.

The authors wish to thank Pat Estergard for her assistance with the project. We also note our debt to our students for making the challenge of teaching this subject such a rewarding one.

WILLIAM M. TABB
ELAINE W. SHOBEN

February 2005

*

ACKNOWLEDGMENT

American Law Institute

*

OUTLINE

---

*

XV

TABLE OF CASES

References are to Pages

C

I

In re (see name of party)

J

K

L

M

N

S

T

U

V

W

Y

REMEDIES

IN A NUTSHELL

*

Chapter 1

INTRODUCTION TO REMEDIES

The study of remedies answers the question that is most important to the victorious party in a law suit: What does a substantive victory mean in practical terms? A plaintiff wants to know about monetary recovery or about an equitable order directed against the defendant. A defendant wants to know about recovery under a bond if a temporary restraining order was wrongfully issued. Both parties want to know about the availability of attorneys' fees, if any, to the prevailing litigant. By definition, a remedy is the means by which rights are enforced or the violation of rights is prevented, redressed or compensated.

The subject of remedies complements the study of both substantive law and procedure. Substantive contract law determines whether or not a valid contract is formed and substantive tort law sets forth standards for negligence. The question of remedies is a second stage inquiry. For example, assuming that a breach of contract has occurred or a tort is established, what sort of relief should the injured party receive and how is that accomplished? Procedural issues may affect that answer. For example, must a claimant post a bond as a condition to obtaining a temporary restraining order? Constitutional issues also may be relevant, such as the doctrine of abstention that restricts the ability of federal courts to enjoin matters in state court proceedings.

Several basic themes recur in the study of remedies. One is the distinction between entitlement and measurement of relief. For example, whether a party may receive attorneys' fees through a federal fee-shifting statute is a question of entitlement, but how those fees are calculated is a measurement issue. Similarly, the nature of the defendant's conduct determines entitlement to the discretionary remedy of punitive damages, but the evidence relevant to assessing punitive damages is a measurement question. Another theme is the interrelation of remedies when there are multiple remedial options in law and equity. For instance, assume that a manufacturing plant is emitting noxious fumes which are causing damage to an orchard located on a neighboring landowner's property. The landowner may successfully maintain an action for nuisance. Remedies may include damages for past and/or future injuries, as well as injunctive relief to prohibit future invasions. The availability of an injunction includes evaluation of many factors: the adequacy of the legal remedies, the irreparable nature of the harm, the balance of hardships, the public interest, and the supervisory role of the court. The subject of remedies explores whether damages, injunctive relief, or both may redress the wrong.

The law of remedies also considers various defenses, limitations, and adjustments to claims. Fundamental issues of fairness between the parties affect all aspects of remedies law.

The interests of third parties, the public, and the courts are also relevant. Similarly, the practicality of framing, enforcing and supervising an injunction influences a court in deciding whether to issue the order and how it might be most effectively written.

There are four basic types or classifications of remedies: (1) coercive remedies, (2) damages, (3) restitution, and (4) declaratory relief. The processes and principles by which the most effective remedies are selected, and the relationship of alternative remedies to each other, are the central themes of this book. First, remedies are defined and limited by the source of the right–statute, common law, or Constitution. (Chapter 2)

(A) Coercive Remedies

Coercive remedies include injunctions (Chapter 3) and specific performance (Chapter 4). They are available only from a court of equity, where a judge determines whether the plaintiff is entitled to the "extraordinary relief" of an order commanding the defendant to do or refrain from doing specific acts. These remedies, like all equitable ones, are subject to the equitable defenses, including unclean hands, laches, estoppel, election of remedies, and unconscionability. (Chapter 5).

Upon a compelling showing by the plaintiff, the court may issue a coercive order even before full trial on the merits. A preliminary injunction gives the plaintiff temporary relief pending trial on the merits. A temporary restraining order affords immediate relief pending the hearing on the preliminary injunction. Both of these types of interlocutory relief are designed to preserve the *status quo* to prevent irreparable harm before a court can decide the substantive merits of the dispute. Such orders are available only upon a strong showing of the necessity for such relief and may be conditioned upon the claimant posting a bond or sufficient security to protect the interests of the defendant in the event that the injunction is later determined to have been wrongfully issued. (Chapter 6)

Injunctions and specific performance remedies are called "coercive" because they are backed by the contempt power. A disobedient defendant can be coerced in several different ways with the contempt power. Incarceration and fines may be imposed, and damages may be awarded to compensate the plaintiff for losses incurred by the willful disobedience of the order. (Chapter 7) They are also characterized as "extraordinary" remedies because courts are hesitant to issue an equitable order that binds a party *in personam* knowing that disobedience of the order could lead to a contempt sanction. As a consequence, equitable orders are deemed subordinated to law, meaning that a type of hierarchy is employed by courts whereby legal remedies are preferred over equitable orders unless the remedy at law is deemed "inadequate" to address the claim asserted.

The traditional injunction is a preventive one, but in the latter part of the twentieth century courts of equity in the United States adapted to modern needs with the development of other types of injunctions in addition to preventive ones: structural, restorative and prophylactic injunctions. A structural injunction, such as a school desegregation order or prison reform order, derives its name from the involvement of the courts in the institutional policies and practices of the defendant entities. A restorative injunction operates to correct the present by undoing the effects of a past wrong, such as by a reinstatement order when an employee has been fired for reasons that violate public policy. It focuses not only prospectively, as does the traditional preventive injunction, but also retroactively. A prophylactic injunction seeks to safeguard the plaintiff's rights by ordering behavior not otherwise required by law so as to minimize the chance that wrongs might recur in the future. (Chapter 8)

Cases involving prior restraints of speech, abatement of nuisances orders, and injunctions against crimes create special problems with fashioning injunctive relief. Common law limitations, constitutional constraints, and legislative enactments have affected the process of judicial discretion in these areas and others. (Chapter 9)

(B) Damages

The damages remedy compensates plaintiffs for losses sustained in violation of their rights. Once a plaintiff has established both the claim in substantive law and the entitlement to a particular type of damages, the problem of measurement remains. For example, what is the proper measure of damages if a contractor fails to follow specifications in building a house? If the parties attempted to set damages in advance through the contract, is the provision enforceable? The law of contract damages governs both questions. (Chapter 10)

Considerations of entitlement and measurement apply also in tort cases. What if a beautiful old tree in front of a house is destroyed by negligence? Is the owner entitled to damages even if the tree did not have any value separate from the land? Is the appropriate measure of damages only any diminution in fair market value of the land, or can damages include the cost of replacement, the loss of enjoyment by the owners, or some other measure? Tort damage law governs. (Chapter 11)

Once the appropriate measure of damages is ascertained, certain adjustments may be made to the award. Courts account for the use and changing value of money by awarding interest and by reducing awards of future losses to present value. (Chapter 12) There are also limitations that the common law imposes on damage awards. They cannot be too remote, speculative, or uncertain. Other forms of limitation come from rules such as the collateral source rule and the doctrine of mitigation or avoidable consequences. Thus, for example, an injured party in a car accident can sue the tortfeasor for medical costs even if those same costs have been paid by insurance. The common law applies this "collateral source" rule regardless of whether the insurance policy provides for subrogation. This rule has been a frequent subject of change by tort reform. Another rule that limits recovery, the avoidable consequences rule, excludes damages that could have been reasonably avoided by the plaintiff, such as exacerbation of injury by failing to seek medical attention in a timely manner. (Chapter 13)

There are also limitations on the types of losses that a plaintiff can claim because not all losses are compensable. There are restrictions on the recovery of mental distress damages and limitations on recovery of purely economic losses. (Chapter 14)

The goal of damage law is compensation and all the topics already noted relate generally to fair compensation for loss. The only exception is punitive damages. Punitive damages are also called exemplary damages or smart money. They function to punish and deter wrongdoers in cases involving egregious conduct. Because these damages play a different societal role under the guise of civil damages, there are constitutional constraints on the ability of states to award them. (Chapter 15)

(C) Restitution

Restitutionary awards have a different goal than compensatory damages. The role of restitution is to restore property to its rightful owner or to disgorge from a defendant any unjust enrichment occasioned by the wrong to the plaintiff. Whereas compensatory damages makes a plaintiff "whole" again after a tort or grants expectancy in contract, the measurement of restitution is the defendant's gains rather than the plaintiff's losses. For example, an embezzler who purchases appreciating collectibles with the misappropriated money is not allowed to keep any profit from the investment. A plaintiff may receive the property itself by imposition of a constructive trust if it is still held by the embezzler. If it has been sold and money profits can be traced, those profits can be received. Because the law of restitution prevents the intentional wrongdoer from profiting from the wrong, the plaintiff thus may receive more than was lost in the original embezzlement.

The animating principle behind restitution is that any windfall should go to an innocent victim rather than be retained by the wrongdoer. As between the innocent victim and the wrongdoer, the windfall goes to the former. The unjust enrichment is disgorged from the defendant and given to the plaintiff. (Chapters 16) There is no disgorgement when the defendant is a bona fide purchaser for value, however, nor when the plaintiff has acted as an officious intermeddler. (Chapter 17)

(D) Attorneys' Fees and Jury Trials

Litigants are affected by two other notable issues related to remedies: the right to a jury and the availability of attorneys' fees. These two topics can dictate important aspects of resolving cases.

The right to a jury trial in federal court is governed by the jurisprudence of the Seventh Amendment. This Constitutional amendment guarantees the right to a jury trial in actions "at law" where the amount in controversy exceeds twenty dollars. The phrase "at law" refers to courts sitting at law rather than in equity. Thus, there is a right to a jury trial in federal legal cases but not equitable ones. Although this amendment does not apply to the states, the states generally follow that same distinction because typically state constitutions have similar provisions. Differences between federal and state law occur in some areas, however, such as cases where there are mixed claims of law and equity. (Chapter 18)

Attorneys' fees, when available, are awarded as "costs" of the suit. The Supreme Court has noted that they are a type of remedy, at least in public interest cases, which give the plaintiff an additional tool for asserting rights. *Evans v. Jeff D.* (S.Ct. 1986). As a general rule, however, attorneys' fees are not recoverable in most claims. The "American Rule" on attorney fees is that parties must bear their own costs of litigation. There are a few common law exceptions to this rule, and several important statutory ones. The major area of statutory change is in the area of civil rights. Further statutory changes have been proposed, including a "loser pays" model. (Chapter 19)

(E) Declaratory Remedies

The purpose of a declaratory remedy is to obtain a declaration of the rights or legal relations between the parties. This remedy is often used to determine the constitutionality of a statute or to construe a private instrument so that the interested parties may obtain a resolution of the dispute at an early stage. Federal and state statutes provide that declaratory relief is to be liberally administered, but the parties must demonstrate a justiciable controversy rather than one of a hypothetical or advisory nature.

Nominal damages also serve to declare the relative rights of the parties. They are awarded when a plaintiff establishes a substantive claim but cannot establish damages. One reason they are important is that nominal damages are sometimes sufficient to support attorneys' fees and punitive damages. Like declaratory judgments, their primary function is to signify rights, such as the right to control property, even in the absence of a substantial remedy. (Chapter 20)

Chapter 2

THE SIGNIFICANCE OF REMEDIAL CHARACTERIZATIONS

The relationship between "rights" and "remedies" is critical to understanding the availability and efficacy of various types of judicial relief. The study of remedies begins with the assumption that the plaintiff has established a substantive right. That right may be (1) based upon a statute, (2) derived from the common law, or (3) permitted directly from the Constitution. There is no question of remedy if the plaintiff does not demonstrate the existence and infringement of a right under one of those sources of law. Beyond that truism, even after the plaintiff prevails with a substantive right, it does not automatically follow that a desired remedy is available for the violation of that particular right. Not every right supports all possible remedies. Just as rights must have a source in the law, remedies also must be derived from common law or statute.

Assuming that one or more remedies is available, a plaintiff must then establish the requirements for the particular remedy. In some instances, a plaintiff may have multiple remedies available for the same operative core of facts. The question then becomes which remedy would be the most effective to address the particular harm presented. For example, if a defendant fraudulently induces a contract for the sale of land, the buyer plaintiff may wish to keep the land and receive damages or may wish to rescind the transaction. If damages are desired, there are two ways to measure compensatory damages. Under the out-of-pocket measure of loss, the plaintiff receives the difference between the contract price and the fair market value of the land. Under the benefit of the bargain approach, the plaintiff receives the difference between the contract price and the value of land if it were as represented, which is usually a higher dollar recovery. If the facts support punitive damages, that award would be in addition to the compensatory damages. If rescission is the remedy, then the parties must make restitution of benefits exchanged. The availability of each of these remedial possibilities turns first on whether the plaintiff prevails with a tort claim or a contract claim or both and then on whether the plaintiff can establish the requirements for each remedy. The difference in the source of rights not only affects these remedies but also affects other practical matters, including the statute of limitations, the availability of attorneys' fees, and the right to a jury trial.

Future chapters examine remedial requirements and evaluate remedial choices. First, this chapter examines (1) the significance of whether a remedy is legal or equitable in nature, and (2) how the source of a right may impose a limitation on the remedy.

(A) Remedies at Law and in Equity

The term "to do equity" in everyday speech implies that a decision-maker has reached a fair and impartial result in a conflict. An "equitable result" usually means a resolution that does not come from established principles but simply derives from common sense and socially acceptable notions of fair play. In the judicial system this popular concept of equity is not the essence of equitable decisionmaking. Instead, "equity" refers to a system of jurisprudence distinguishable from the system "at law." Each have their own specific characteristics and attributes, even following the merger of law and equity in modern law. Although the judge sitting in equity has discretion whether to allow a particular remedy, that process is guided by principles established by *stare decisis*.

The origin of equity as a separate system of law began in fourteenth century England. The King's common law courts were incapable of doing justice in some circumstances because of the procedures and writs. Not all litigants could conform their cases to the rigidity of the pleading requirements. Alternative relief was sought from the King's Chancellor, who had greater freedom to do justice. For example, a suitor could seek relief from the King, through his Chancellor, from fraud. Because the common law did not recognize fraud as a defense to a contract under seal, the contract would be enforceable but for the Chancellor's intervention. See Ellen E. Sward, "A History of the Civil Trial in the United States," 51 U. Kan. L. Rev. 347 (2003). With the increase in such claims, equity became a separate court system that afforded relief to petitioners who had no adequate remedy at law because of some harsh legal doctrine.

The King's Chancellor did not provide remedies in the same manner as the courts of the King's Bench. As a religious figure, the Chancellor operated on the conscience of the defendant. Thus, equity had jurisdiction over the person of the defendant rather than his property and could jail disobedient defendants. In modern law, equity similarly enforces its orders through the contempt power.

The Seventh Amendment of the Constitution provides that there is a right to trial by jury for causes "at law." There is no similar right to trial by jury for actions in equity. In the federal system, this constitutional right has been interpreted to mean that causes of action seeking legal remedies as opposed to equitable ones must be afforded trial by jury. An action seeking only equitable remedies may be tried by the judge without a jury, although an advisory jury can be impaneled.

The cases entertained by Chancery historically fell into two main categories: (1) those where the suitor had some remedy at law, but not an adequate one, and (2) those where a remedy at law was unavailable because the cause of action was not one recognized at law. In modern law, the first category is reflected in cases where the suitor seeks an equitable remedy such as an injunction or specific performance on the grounds that the damages remedy at law is inadequate. "Inadequacy" has a special meaning in the law of equity because it is a shorthand expression for the policy that equitable remedies are subordinate to legal ones. They are subordinate in the sense that the damage remedy is preferred in any individual case if it is adequate. Although scholars have attacked this rule as outdated, the usual policy reasons for it are judicial efficiency and fairness. The efficiency argument notes that equitable remedies generally require more judicial supervision and the fairness argument is based on the fact that equity acts *in personam* on the defendant and punishes disobedience with contempt.

The second category of cases before the Chancellor in old England was those where the King's Courts would not recognize the action. In modern law, this category is called "substantive equity." Equitable trusts and liens, as well as stockholders' derivative actions, are notable examples of this category. There is a split among jurisdictions concerning the availability of a jury trial in cases involving substantive equity if the remedies sought are otherwise legal ones. The Supreme Court held in *Ross v. Bernhard* (S.Ct.1970) that in federal courts, the nature of the remedy controls the right to a jury trial rather than the historical accident of a claim being one of substantive equity. Most states have elected not to follow the federal approach and retain the old rule that claims in substantive equity do not support a right to a jury trial.

Historically some petitioners came to equity for protection from the legal enforcement of contracts. Equity was the original source of concepts such as promissory estoppel and unconscionability. Today those historically equitable doctrines have been incorporated into legal jurisprudence as well. Despite the diminished importance of recognizing the substantive contributions of equity, the concept of equitable remedies distinct from legal ones remains important. Equitable remedies include flexible coercive orders such as injunctions and specific performance orders. Some restitutionary remedies are equitable, such as constructive trusts or rescission and restitution in contract. The hallmark of equity is discretion. Courts retain considerable discretion both with respect to determining if an equitable order should be issued and also how it should be fashioned.

The most prevalent legal remedy is damages. Some restitutionary remedies are also legal, such as quasi-contract. In a merged system of law and equity, a plaintiff may seek both legal and equitable remedies in the same claim. The importance of the distinction between legal and equitable remedies, however, lies with the availability of a jury trial. The Supreme Court held in *Dairy Queen, Inc. v. Wood* (S.Ct.1962) that if a plaintiff presents a mixed claim of law and equity, the legal issues must be tried first by the jury and any remaining equitable issues may be tried by the judge in a manner not

inconsistent with the jury verdict. Both plaintiffs
and defendants possess jury trial rights, which may
be waived.

In the state court systems the right to trial by
jury is often different. The Seventh Amendment has
not been held to apply to the states. Some states
have constitutional provisions of their own affecting
the right, but others rely entirely upon historical
precedent. Cases in which the plaintiff seeks only
legal remedies usually entitle the parties to trial by
jury; cases seeking only equitable remedies do not.
In a merged state court system, a mixed claim of
legal and equitable remedies may not entitle the
parties to a jury trial if the primary character of the
case is equitable. The doctrine of "equitable clean-
up" may control whereby the judge as trier of fact
in equity may decide also any incidental damages
issues.

(B) Limitations on Remedies

Once the plaintiff has established a substantive
right, the available remedy will be based upon the
same source. That source may impose limitations on
the remedy itself. Consider the provision governing
unconscionable contracts in the Uniform Commercial Code. Section § 2–302 provides:

> If the court as a matter of law finds the contract
> or any clause of the contract to have been uncon-
> scionable at the time it was made the court may
> refuse to enforce the contract, or it may enforce
> the remainder of the contract without the uncon-
> scionable clause, or it may so limit the application

of any unconscionable clause to avoid any unconscionable result.

The remedy here is a limited one. The court may refuse enforcement of all or part of an unconscionable contract but it may not grant compensatory or punitive damages that may otherwise be justified. In *Cowin Equipment Co. v. General Motors Corp.* (11th Cir.1984) the plaintiff was a car dealer who tried to sue the manufacturer for losses occasioned by its refusal to let the dealer return cars that the dealer couldn't sell during a recession. The dealer alleged that the no-return clause was unconscionable and that as a result of the manufacturer's enforcement of that clause the dealer suffered losses when it had to sell the cars below cost. The court held that regardless of any unconscionability in the provision, the remedy sought was not permissible under the statute. Damages were not available even if they flowed directly from the claim.

An action at common law typically permits the plaintiff to recover any type of common law remedy. Remedial efficacy is relevant to a court's consideration of whether to permit a new cause of action at common law. If a meaningful remedy cannot be afforded in the usual case, then the jurisdiction may consider that problem as a reason to deny expansion of common law duties. Many states include this reason as a justification for denying claims for educational malpractice, for example.

Similarly, claims brought directly under the federal Constitution support all common law remedies.

For several policy reasons including the expansiveness of the remedies, courts do not permit such claims when there are other avenues of redress.

The relationship between rights and remedies is circular in the sense that a right is only as great as its remedy and remedies are limited by the rights they protect. Thus, for example, when the legislature creates a new statutory right and defines a remedy such as $500 per violation, then the right might be repeatedly violated if the wrongdoer is willing to pay the limited amount of damages. Unless the court is willing to expand the remedies beyond the statutory scheme and allow for an injunction, the right is diminished by the remedial limitation.

Most courts are unwilling to assume that a legislature intended for courts to expand upon a specific statutory provision, such as the $500 remedy in the previous example. One case which famously was willing to do so is *Orloff v. Los Angeles Turf Club* (Cal.1947). In that case a California statute prohibited racial discrimination in certain public places and provided simply for a damage remedy. This statute predated Congressional action in the Civil Rights Act of 1964 which ended racial segregation in public places as a matter of federal law. The California case arose almost twenty years before and the issue was whether the court should permit an injunction against a race track that wanted to discriminate on the basis of race in admission. The California Supreme Court ignored the literal wording of the remedial provision in order to give effect to the apparent purpose of the legislature. There was no other way, the court reasoned, for the objects of the Civil Code to be effectuated and justice promoted–goals also required under California law. By issuing an injunction that bound the defendant *in personam*, the court could ensure compliance with the law. An award of damages would not necessarily affect future behavior because a liable party could theoretically continue to violate rights and simply pay compensation for the resulting harm. In contrast, disobedience of the equitable order could trigger sanctions through the contempt power of the court. This case illustrates the general principle that a right without a meaningful remedy is a "paper tiger" which cannot vindicate a violation.

Remedies are also limited and defined by procedure. A remedy is more effective in some situations if a class action is permissible to provide redress widely. Congress famously limited remedies through a denial of jurisdiction to federal courts in matters of labor disputes. The Norris–LaGuardia Act prohibits federal courts from issuing injunctions in such cases. The Supreme Court explained in *Boys Markets, Inc. v. Retail Clerks Union* (S.Ct.1970):

The Norris–LaGuardia Act was responsive to a situation totally different from that which exists today. In the early part of this century, the federal courts generally were regarded as allies of management in its attempt to prevent the organization and strengthening of labor unions; and in this industrial struggle the injunction became a potent weapon that was wielded against the activities of labor groups. * * * Congress, therefore, determined initially to limit severely the power of the federal courts to issue injunctions in any case involving or growing out of any labor dispute * * *.

Courts have had to interpret this limitation on federal jurisdiction in light of other federal statutes that grant jurisdiction over related matters. The general principle, however, is that the legislature may limit the discretion of courts through statute.

Chapter 3

PREVENTIVE INJUNCTIONS

The classic form of injunction in private litigation is the preventive injunction. By definition, a preventive injunction is a court order designed to avoid future harm to a party by prohibiting or mandating certain behavior by another party. The injunction is "preventive" in the sense of avoiding harm. The wording may be either prohibitory ("Do not trespass") or mandatory ("Remove the obstruction").

The traditional requirements for a preventive injunction are the subject of this chapter. Recall that a precondition for asserting any remedy is that the plaintiff must have established the substantive claim. For purposes of equitable relief, the right can stem from statute, common law, or constitutional sources. Modern equity will act to protect both personal as well as property interests, although historically equity required plaintiffs to demonstrate a property interest.

The traditional requirements for a preventive injunction are: (1) inadequacy of the remedy at law, (2) irreparable harm, (3) balance of hardships, and (4) public interest. Additional considerations include the imminency of the harm and the practicality of supervision.

(A) Inadequacy of the Remedy at Law and Irreparable Harm

The term "equity jurisdiction" refers to the appropriate exercise of a court's discretion in granting equitable relief. The first element of equity jurisdiction is the inadequacy of the remedy at law. History explains the rule better than logic, but the rule still has force to restrict the availability of equitable remedies. The inadequacy rule was originally applied by the Chancellor in the sixteenth century to determine whether to take a case or to leave the petitioner to go to the law courts with a writ for relief. *See* W. Blackstone, *Commentaries* 46–55; F. Maitland, *Equity* 7 (1930). In modern law, courts frequently invoke the rule as a shorthand explanation for granting or denying equitable relief. In cases involving interests in real property, for example, it is the uniqueness of each parcel of land that makes damages inadequate to compensate losses.

The use of the word "jurisdiction" by modern courts is confusing because it does not refer to the power of the court in the way that subject matter jurisdiction and personal jurisdiction concern the court's power. Although there was an historical justification for the use of the term "jurisdiction" by the Chancery, the term "equity jurisdiction" refers to the appropriateness of equitable relief as a matter of remedial equity. Thus, if a court incorrectly concludes that equitable relief should be granted, it is merely an erroneous order that must be appealed and not a void order from a court lacking jurisdiction. *See* Z. Chafee, Jr., *Some Problems of Equity* 296–336 (1950).

The first aspect of equity jurisdiction is that the remedy at law must be inadequate. That requirement is met if damages would be too speculative or if multiple damage actions would be necessary because of the nature of the invasion of the plaintiff's rights. In one well-known case an injunction was granted to require the defendant to remove great boulders which he had left on the plaintiff's property beyond the term of the license to do so. The plaintiff could not easily remove the boulders and sue for the cost of removal of the trespassing rocks because of their size and weight. Wheelock v. Noonan (N.Y.1888). In contrast, the remedy at law is adequate if the defendant left litter on the property because the plaintiff can pay for someone to remove the trash and then sue the defendant for the cost incurred. Connor v. Grosso (Cal.1953).

When there is a continuing trespass that the plaintiff cannot remove with self-help, the property owner could sue for damages measured by the rental value of the land. This remedy is inadequate to prevent future invasions, however, if the defendant were willing to pay the damages in order to continue use of plaintiff's land. The defendant thus would become the forced tenant of an unwilling landlord unless an injunction forces an end to the trespass. In such a situation, the multiplicity of actions that would be required to compensate the landowner would be the articulated basis for meeting the inadequacy rule. To establish the inadequacy of the remedy at law on the basis of a multiplicity of actions for continuing trespass, the plaintiff must show that the defendant will not honor a demand to vacate. For example, an injunction was appropriate under this rule when a patient would not vacate a hospital room because her husband refused repeated demands to transfer her to a nursing home. *See* Lucy Webb Hayes National Training School for Deaconesses and Missionaries v. Geoghegan (D.D.C. 1967).

In contrast to continuing trespasses, a pattern of *repeated* trespasses requires a showing that the defendant is likely to continue to repeat the invasions in knowing violation of the plaintiff's rights. Otherwise the remedy at law is adequate because the plaintiff can sue for damages for the past trespass. Such repeated violations have been shown likely to recur in one case where a neighbor's construction project kept knocking into the neighbor's hedge and in another where a duck hunter made annual trespasses on neighboring land. *See* Thomas v. Weller (Neb.1979); Phillips v. Wertz (Tex.Civ. App.1977).

Other special circumstances warrant extraordinary relief as well on the grounds that law cannot provide an adequate remedy because of the nature of the right involved. Constitutional claims, such as for school desegregation, involve rights that require equitable intervention. The Supreme Court discussed the necessity of flexible equitable powers in its second opinion in *Brown v. Board of Education* (S.Ct.1955) addressing remedial issues for the correction of the violation of equal protection where public schools were intentionally segregated on the basis of race. Similarly, equity intervenes to correct unconstitutional situations such prison systems that violate the Eighth Amendment guarantee against cruel and unusual punishment. *See* Hutto v. Finney (S.Ct.1978).

Other types of interests are routinely found to support equitable intervention because of the inadequacy of legal remedies. Nuisance cases are often said to support injunctions as the "usual" remedy, particularly where the nuisance is of a public character and affects health and safety. Similarly, cases involving intangible business interests, such as the unauthorized use of customer lists, often support equitable relief because damages are speculative and irreparable harm results.

Most jurisdictions list irreparable harm as a second, separate requirement for coercive relief, but this element is often subsumed in the inadequacy rule. As a general matter, the remedy at law is inadequate precisely because the harm is irreparable and damages do not suffice.

The requirement of irreparable harm, however, does play a distinguishable role. Such harm must be great in nature and not trivial. Some interests are routinely protected by equity, such as injunctions against trespass to land, because of the inadequacy of the remedy at law. The irreparable harm requirement, however, prevents the court from exercising its extraordinary powers in equity if the harm involved is trivial. An irreparable harm also may be seen as one which is qualitative in nature, such as involving invasion of privacy claims in tort.

There is another class of cases to which the inadequacy rule does not apply. Claims invoking substantive equity, as opposed to remedial equity, may be brought without regard to the adequacy of the remedy at law. Substantive equity allows a cause of action in equity for certain types of interests like trusts, mortgages, bankruptcy, and stockholders' derivative actions. Historically these interests were recognized only in Chancery, as described in Chapter 2, so there was no further consideration of the adequacy of the remedy at law. In contrast, remedial equity refers to cases where the subject matter of the claim could be brought at law, such as for tort or breach of contract, but the remedy sought is available only in equity.

(B) Imminency

Courts will order equitable relief only when the threatened harm is imminent. If the harm has already occurred and is not reasonably likely to reoccur, then a court will decline to issue an injunction. The reason is that the order would not serve a useful purpose to prohibit future conduct and the damages remedy at law can compensate for any injury suffered. Conversely, equity will not act to prohibit future harm that is considered remote or speculative. Courts do not issue "be good" orders but instead require proof of immediate and probable harm. This limitation avoids wasting judicial resources, but it also protects the defendant. Because equitable orders are backed by the contempt power, an individual who commits a wrong such as trespass faces a greater potential penalty from violating a prohibitory injunction than the usual criminal and civil sanctions for the wrong.

In contrast both to harm already completed and to an unsubstantiated threat of future harm, imminent harm is an invasion that is likely to occur soon unless there is equitable intervention. If the conduct sought to be enjoined has been ongoing, such as continuous pollution of neighboring lands by a factory, the claimant can prove the necessary immediacy of the harm by pointing to the continuous invasion of their interests.

The more difficult applications of imminency involve cases where a defendant has intermittently engaged in behavior that infringes upon a legally protected right of the plaintiff. The defendant is not doing anything at the time the plaintiff goes to court, but the plaintiff can demonstrate a likely invasion in the near future either on the basis of past behavior or on other grounds. For example, if a defendant has engaged in a pattern of parking on the plaintiff's property regularly, the likelihood of repeated trespass is shown from the pattern. It is also relevant whether the plaintiff has communicated a request to stop trespassing because otherwise the defendant may not repeat the trespass once on notice of the plaintiff's objection. An injunction must be based on the court's prediction that harm is imminently likely to occur, so the plaintiff must establish a basis for that probability.

The plaintiff's demonstration of probable future invasion is even more difficult when the pattern of past invasions has been varied and unpredictable. An illustration is *Galella v. Onassis* (S.D.N.Y.1972). In that case, the wife of the former president of the United States sought an injunction to restrain a professional free-lance photographer from violating her rights of privacy. The evidence showed that the photographer had repeatedly engaged in harassing behavior of the Onassis family in order to obtain pictures, but each time the invasive behavior was different. Based upon the pattern of past conduct, the court concluded that the photographer's behavior would continue indefinitely in the future. The evidence of imminency was very strong because the photographer had even sent an advertisement to customers announcing future anticipated pictures of Onassis. Even though the pattern of behavior was varied in the types of invasive conduct, the overall nature of it was harassing. With sufficient evidence, even an unpredictable pattern can establish imminency.

(C) Balance of Hardships and Public Interest

Injunctions are discretionary and not a matter of right. In the exercise of that discretion, a judge weighs the relative hardships of the parties, considers any problems of practicality in enforcing an order, and public interest. These factors, along with the determination of the inadequacy of the remedy

at law and irreparable harm, form the "equities" of
the case. The trial judge's assessment of the equities is upheld on appeal unless there has been an
abuse of discretion.

The factors of practicality and hardship can affect
the case in two ways. First, they are elements in the
determination of the equities. No injunction will
issue unless it is practical to do so and unless the
balance of hardships tips in favor of the plaintiff.
The judge weighs the relative hardships–how much
the plaintiff would benefit by the injunction against
the burden to the defendant. Second, the judge may
consider practicality and hardship in determining
the scope of the order. In a nuisance case, for
example, the court may order limited abatement;
offensive animals may be reduced in number but
not eliminated or noise may be restricted during
certain hours. The question, then, is not whether a
hardship can be entirely avoided or eliminated but
rather which party should bear the burden and
why.

The burden on the defendant is often economic,
but it need not be a dollar loss. Justice Cardozo
explained in *Yome v. Gorman* (N.Y.1926) that it is
not possible to formulate a rule but only to "exem-
plify a process." In that case the plaintiff sought to
move the remains of loved ones from one cemetery
to another after a change in her religious affiliation.
The interests involved could not be quantified in
any objective way and the judge was required to
balance the sentiments as much as possible.

Another example of a noneconomic burden that a court must balance is a restraint on speech. The value of what is protected by the injunction must be balanced against the value of the First Amendment. The Supreme Court considered such an injunction against abortion protestors at a health clinic in *Madsen v. Women's Health Center, Inc.* (S.Ct.1994). The Court held that an injunction restraining the speech is permissible if the rights of the parties are carefully balanced and the injunction narrowly tailored. It is Constitutional for states to issue injunctions that protect a woman's freedom to seek lawful medical and counseling services, but such injunctions must also protect the protestors' right of speech. The injunction in that case established a 36–foot buffer zone around the clinic and surrounding private property. It also imposed limited noise restrictions and provided for a 300–foot no-approach zone. The Court held that the provisions establishing the buffer zone around the clinic and noise restrictions did not violate the First Amendment, but that the buffer zone on private property and the no-approach zone burdened more speech than necessary.

The public interest also affects the decision whether to grant an injunction as well as the scope and nature of it. Relevant considerations are public health and safety as well as public economic interests. The public interest in the continued operation of a major employer was relevant in the famous case of *Boomer v. Atlantic Cement Co.* (N.Y.1970). In this case landowners sued a neighboring cement plant for injury from its pollution. Under New York law, an injunction was the usual remedy for nuisance, but the problem here was the potential injury to the larger community because of the corresponding loss in jobs.

The court in *Boomer* declined to enjoin the multimillion dollar operation and instead conditioned an injunction on the failure of the defendant to pay the plaintiffs permanent damages. The practical effect of this approach was to allow only damages and no equitable relief. The dissenting opinion characterized the result as an inappropriate inverse condemnation because the permanent damages allowed the company a "servitude on the land" to continue its pollution. The taking of property for public purposes, the dissenting judge reasoned, is appropriate only when the public is primarily served in the taking or impairment of property and he saw no such public use or benefit in allowing a company to continue to pollute.

Boomer is a favorite topic of authors in the area of law and economics, who generally approve the result. In the absence of a court order specifying the amount that the company must pay the landowners, the parties could negotiate the amount that the landowners would take in exchange for the right of the company to pollute them. Theoretically, if the pollution were very significant, the amount of money necessary to purchase the right to pollute would be so high that excessive polluters would be driven out of business by the market force.

The court in *Boomer* refused to grant an injunction that would have enjoined the operation of the nuisance unless the pollution were abated within eighteen months. The court noted that if there were no new technological advances in that time to allow the abatement within reasonable cost, the landowners would be in the position to extort an unreasonable settlement. If the company elected instead to close at the end of the eighteen months, the community would lose an important part of its economy.

Public interest can be demonstrated by statute as well as under common law. In some situations, both parties can point to public interest factors that favor their position. For example, in *Boomer* the factory argued successfully that their operation serves the public interest by contributing jobs and taxes to the local economy. The competing public interest was the environmental pollution and widespread interference with neighboring landowners. This 1970 opinion slightly predated the era of federal legislative activism in environmental law. The strong public interest in the environment is now reflected in numerous statutes.

Chapter 4

SPECIFIC PERFORMANCE

Specific performance is an equitable discretionary remedy that is issued to enforce contractual rights and duties. The normative remedy for breach of contract is damages, so specific performance requires a showing that the claimant's rights and expectations pursuant to the agreement necessitates equitable intervention. The role of the court in ordering prospective performance is simply to carry out the original bargain intended by the parties. The remedy, like other types of injunctions, binds the party enjoined *in personam*. Therefore, disobedience of the equitable order may be punishable by contempt . Specific performance is available both at common law and, in a liberalized form, under the Uniform Commercial Code governing transactions involving the sale of goods. The equitable defenses, like laches and unclean hands, may preclude specific performance. If specific performance is denied, the non-breaching party may still seek any available legal remedies.

Courts consider several basic requirements in deciding the propriety of specific performance: (1) the existence of a valid contract with definite and certain terms, (2) the plaintiff is able and ready to perform their own duties and has satisfied all conditions under the agreement, (3) the breaching party is able to render performance, (4) no adequate remedy at law exists, and (5) the balance of interests and relative hardships favors the claimant. Additionally, the court will take into account potential problems in supervision or enforcement of the order.

(A) Definite and Certain Terms

The contract terms must be definite and certain in order for a court to issue a specific performance order. This requirement must be distinguished from the level of definiteness required to support a finding of contract formation. A higher level of certainty and definiteness of terms is required, then, as a predicate for specific performance than for damages at law. The reasons for the elevated role of certainty in equity are to aid the court in framing the decree and to ensure that the party enjoined understands with appropriate clarity the nature of the obligations expected. The latter consideration is critical because disobedience of the order could subject the party to potential contempt sanctions. Therefore, if significant contract terms are considered vague or ambiguous and not capable of reasonable interpretation through resort to extrinsic evidence, the court will decline equitable relief. In some cases, a court may supply a missing term, such as time for delivery or total quantity in an output contract, and authorize specific performance to carry out the parties' expectations. *See* U.C.C. § 2–716 comment 2.

(B) Ability to Perform

A order for specific performance will only be issued upon a showing that it will serve a useful purpose and that both parties are able to satisfactorily perform remaining contractual duties. Claimants, as a matter of fairness, must also show that they have completed all of their own duties under the contract. If a defendant is unable to comply with the order, such as where the subject matter of the contract already has been transferred to a bona fide purchaser or substantially destroyed, then an equitable decree would be futile.

(C) Inadequate Remedy at Law

The most important factor affecting the decision with respect to specific performance typically is whether an award of damages would constitute an adequate legal remedy. The preference for legal remedies over equitable orders exists for several reasons. First, since a specific performance order is essentially a specialized type of injunction, the doctrine of subordination of equitable remedies is followed. Equity is seen as a harsher avenue of relief because it binds parties *in personam*. Also, equitable orders may require more extensive judicial resources of supervision and enforcement. Finally, the nature of contract bargaining itself reflects a strong sense that parties ordinarily expect either performance or payment as a substitution for lost performance. The theory of efficient breach of contract provides that it maximizes economic resources to allow a party to breach and pay damages for losses caused by the breach in order to move goods to a higher bidder. An equitable order commanding a breaching party to perform, then, must overcome the traditional contract view of seeing damages as the norm for breach.

The circumstances in which damages or other legal remedies would not constitute an "adequate" remedy include the difficulties of obtaining a reasonable substitute, proving damages with reasonable certainty, or of collecting the damages awarded. See Restatement (Second) of Contracts § 360. For example, if the non-breaching party cannot reasonably obtain a replacement for the subject matter of the contract and has an objectively justifiable basis for expecting performance, then equitable relief may be appropriate. The most common illustration of this principle is the historical view that land is a proper subject for specific performance because each parcel of land is unique. Other non-fungible items, such as heirlooms or items that are scarce but important to the claimant, also may be deemed unique in the qualitative sense.

The purpose and expectations of the parties in the bargain are also relevant in deciding adequacy of legal remedies. For instance, if a buyer of certain property is a dealer and has a primary interest in reselling for a profit, a court may decide that the expectation interest may adequately satisfied with a money judgment. On the other hand, if the buyer of land planned to occupy and farm the tract of land, then the court may readily conclude that the property was unique and irreplaceable and order specific performance.

(D) Balance of Hardships

The court, in the exercise of its discretion, will balance the equities and relative hardships of the parties in deciding the propriety of specific performance. Whether the order is issued or denied one party will presumably experience some degree of hardship. Thus, the question is the relative degree of the burden on the parties and how equities affect which party should bear the hardship.

A variety of factors may be considered in the balancing calculus, including the extent of judicial supervision and enforcement that may be required. Also, the court may consider whether the contract potentially implicates third party contracts or the public interest. Finally, the court may deny specific performance in situations involving mistake, grossly disproportionate consideration, duress, or other unreasonable hardship. Even if those factors may not rise to the level of independently avoiding the contract as a matter of substantive law, they may influence the court's discretion in granting or shaping equitable relief.

For example, although substantive contract law does not inquire into the adequacy of consideration for purposes of contract formation, a significant disparity in consideration exchanged can affect equitable relief. The court may not invalidate the contract as unconscionable, yet may determine that damages would adequately compensate for a breach rather than impose equitable relief to enforce a hard bargain. The evaluation of the reasonableness of the consideration exchanged is made at the time of contracting rather than based upon subsequent events.

Similarly, a unilateral mistake of fact made by one contracting party may influence a court to decline equitable relief if the effect of the order would heavily burden the mistaken party. Although the mistake may not be sufficient to prevent formation of the contract, it may affect equitable discretion. The sympathy of a court with respect to consideration of a mistake is heightened where it was caused by misrepresentations by the other contracting party. Restatement (Second) Contracts § 364(1)(a).

Finally, a court will consider potential problems associated with supervising a complex equitable decree. If the court would incur a significant burden of time and resources or if the nature of the subject matter affected by the decree calls for technical expertise, a court may decide that damages are a more appropriate remedy. See Restatement (Second) of Contracts § 366.

(E) Fashioning Relief

In the exercise of equitable discretion, courts will weigh a litany of factors both with respect to determining entitlement to specific performance as well as the manner in which the order is framed. Even where a claimant has demonstrated lack of an adequate remedy at law, the court may still choose to decline equitable relief entirely or limit its effect based upon other considerations. A court will try to approximate, as closely as possible, the balance of respective rights and duties embodied in the original contract. In certain cases, however, a party cannot deliver the exact performance bargained for but the non-breaching party still seeks specific performance. An illustration of the problem is where a seller in a land sales contract does not possess complete title to the full acreage subject to the contract.

Several remedial options exist for the court in such situations, each of which will carry out the intentions of the parties. For a minor discrepancy that does not impair the contract substantially, the court may find that no breach has occurred and still order specific performance with no adjustment in price. If the court finds a slight defect, it may decree specific performance with an abatement in the purchase price proportionate to the deficiency. Where the defect is considered substantial, either quantitatively or qualitatively, the court may award damages for the breach or order rescission and restitution. A specific performance order may be inappropriate if it requires a major rewriting of the contract.

(F) Mutuality of Remedy

One historical impediment to the availability of specific performance was lack of mutuality of remedy. The rule held that specific performance would only be available to one party if it was equally available to the other contracting party. The mutuality of remedy argument rests on a pure fiction in that it asks a theoretical question of the availability of a remedy if the other party had been in breach. Although the symmetry and apparent fairness of the doctrine reflected equity's traditions of justice, the rule worked unsatisfactorily in certain instances. Also, the doctrine fails to consider that parties bargain for different things.

For example, if parties contracted to convey land in exchange for services rather than money, the mutuality rule could potentially foreclose specific performance in the event of a breach. An illustration of the application of the mutuality doctrine is shown in *Henderson v. Fisher* (Cal.App.1965). In that case, an 86 year old man named Baker contracted to convey a deed to his home in exchange for receiving care and support from the plaintiffs during his lifetime. At the time of making the contract Baker was in reasonably good health. The plaintiffs moved into the home and provided the personal services contemplated by the agreement but Baker died just 18 days later. The trial court denied the plaintiff's claim for specific performance of the realty, partially on the basis that the contract lacked mutuality, but granted a small sum under quantum meruit. The rationale was that since constitutional restraints against involuntary servitude would prevent the seller from hypothetically obtaining an equitable decree to demand performance of personal services, then the remedy was also unavailable to force conveyance of the land. The appellate court reversed, finding that the mutuality rule did not apply when the contract was fully performed.

The case reflects a growing dissatisfaction by courts with the potential for hardship or inequity resulting from strict adherence to the rule. Courts have recognized various exceptions to the rule or simply rejected it completely. As illustrated in *Henderson v. Fisher*, the mutuality rule did not apply when the contract was fully executed. Other exceptions are where the party seeking specific performance had substantially performed or the court was assured of continued performance in the future. Also, some courts limited the rule to the time equitable relief was sought rather than when the contract was formed. Several states have enacted statutes which codified the developing common law limitations on the mutuality rule. A companion doctrine that historically affected contract formation, mutuality of obligation, was also expressly rejected by Restatement (Second) Contracts § 79.

The modern view treats mutuality of remedies as just one factor in deciding the propriety of specific performance. Courts may consider mutuality to ensure that both sides will fully perform if an equitable order is given. *See* Restatement (Second) Contracts § 363 comment c. In that sense, the doctrine provides security to the party in breach that they will not be compelled to perform without adequate assurance of receiving return performance from the non-breaching party. In summary, because parties typically have different expectations in the bargain, courts no longer require that the remedies potentially available to them must correspond or mirror each other.

(G) Personal Services

The traditional rule in equity is that courts will not order specific performance of contracts for personal services, such as contracts with professional athletes or artistic performers. Several policy considerations support this judicial approach: (1) an adequate remedy at law exists unless the services are unique, (2) such orders are difficult to supervise and enforce, and (3) and the constitutional prohibition of involuntary servitude. Practical problems of fashioning an order with sufficient specificity would also be critical since the decree would be enforceable with contempt. Moreover, courts are disinclined to force someone to work in a hostile environment. Similarly, employers are rarely required to accept personal services tendered under a contract unless subject to a statutory requirement, such as in fair employment acts.

Although equity will not compel performance of personal services, the court may grant a negative injunction to prohibit rendering the same services for another. In the leading case, *Lumley v. Wagner* (Ch.1852), an opera singer entered into an exclusive contract to sing for the proprietor of a London theater for a period of three months. Another London theater persuaded the singer to break the contract and perform for their opera production instead. The court granted an injunction restraining her from performing for the competing production.

On appeal, the Lord Chancellor upheld the prohibitory injunction, but acknowledged that the court could not force compliance with the original contract.

The reasoning supporting issuance of a negative injunction to protect the contractual bargain is that damages are considered an inadequate remedy at law. The inadequacy requirement may be met both by the reference to the difficulty in measuring the harm and also by the inability to obtain a suitable substitute performer because of the special skills involved. The non-breaching party cannot use equity to compel performance, but may only restrain the breaching party from performing under another contract.

Restrictive covenants are commonly included in various employment contracts and may support issuance of negative injunctions, provided they are deemed reasonable in subject matter, geographic coverage, and time period specified. Such restrictive covenants may also be implied. The Restatement (Second) of Contracts § 367, comment b, states that the character of a personal service is one which is "non-delegable", meaning that the contracting party has certain unique abilities to perform the contractual obligations. If those duties were delegated or assigned to a third party, the non-breaching party would not receive the benefit of their bargain.

(H) Uniform Commercial Code

The Uniform Commercial Code § 2–716(1) provides that specific performance may be an appropriate remedy when goods are "unique or in other proper circumstances." The Code espouses a "more liberal attitude" than common law with respect to authorizing equitable relief. See § 2–716, U.C.C., Comment 1. The rationale for expanding the availability of specific performance may reflect the recognition that such commercial transactions are generally between relatively sophisticated parties and that replacement goods may be difficult to obtain through cover.

The concept of "uniqueness" carries forward in restated fashion the common law tradition of considering whether the non-breaching party has an adequate remedy at law. Therefore, goods may satisfy the test of uniqueness where no commercially reasonable substitute is readily available without undue expense, difficulty, or delay. Other factors that may suggest uniqueness could include difficulties in valuation, prospective problems in collection of damages, and the potential of multiplicity of suits to obtain the benefit of the bargain. Most commonly, however, the critical factor is whether or not the non-breaching party can enter the market and obtain cover to replace the contract goods. Where goods are relatively fungible, such as most commodities, damages would ordinarily be a satisfactory remedy for breach of contract.

The comments to section 2–716 admonish that the test of uniqueness must be made based upon the "total situation which characterizes the contract." See comment 2, § 2–716. For example, output and requirements contracts are acknowledged

as potentially proper subjects for specific performance because alternate sources or markets are not
readily available.

The general term "in other proper circumstances" expresses the broader application of the
standard for equitable relief. This alternative portion of the test amplifies the issue of uniqueness
and also considers the type of contract involved.
Comment 2 to § 2–716 suggests that the buyer's
inability to cover serves as strong evidence of "other proper circumstances" and may justify specific
performance. For example, in *Kaiser Trading Co. v.
Associated Metals & Minerals Corp.* (N.D.Cal.1970)
the court found that because the subject matter of
the contract was a scarce material, the buyer could
not readily cover. Further, since the material was
an important substance used in the company's manufacturing process, damages would not be an adequate remedy and specific performance was necessary to protect its expectation interest. Also, in
Eastern Air Lines, Inc. v. Gulf Oil Corp. (S.D.Fla.
1975), the court recognized the problems associated
with product shortages and specifically enforced a
contract for supplying aviation fuel to an airline
company during the 1973 Arab oil embargo.

Chapter 5

EQUITABLE DEFENSES

This chapter concerns defenses that a defendant may raise to equitable relief. Such defenses are independent of any defense to the substantive claim itself, such as privilege. Recall that to obtain an equitable order a plaintiff must first establish the substantive claim for a right to relief and then must establish the requirements for the equitable order itself, as seen in Chapters 3 and 4.

The equitable defenses covered in this chapter are laches, unclean hands, estoppel, unconscionability, and election of remedies. They share a common origin in the old English courts of equity as reflected in the Chancellor's laws of conscience. The Chancellor would not give relief to a suitor whose behavior was somehow "tainted" with respect to the claim. The Chancellor had discretion to deny equitable relief if the claimant had engaged in unconscionable or otherwise wrongful conduct in securing the right being asserted, or if the defendant had been prejudiced by prior inconsistent conduct or by undue delay by the suitor in pursuing the claim. In such cases, the plaintiff would be sent from equity back to law to seek whatever damages remedy was available for the substantive right in dispute. Even in a case where the defendant's behavior was much worse by comparison, the Chancellor was unsupportive of rights tainted by improper conduct and the plaintiff would be sent to seek redress from a court of law. One principle that remains in modern law is that a court sitting in equity will not sully itself by lending aid to someone who has a questionable moral posture with regard to the claim. Another central principle is that the court maintains considerable discretion to grant, deny, or shape equitable relief based upon reference to the claimant's own conduct, even where a claim might be otherwise meritorious.

These defenses in modern equity still have a moralistic foundation; a court will not grant equitable relief if the plaintiff has behaved in a way prejudicial to the defendant or offensive to public policy. As in the past, there is no entitlement to equitable relief, and these defenses have been preserved even in the merged system of law and equity. Modern equity is guided by discretion that is more constrained by principles of *stare decisis* than the Chancellor's original courts of equity, but its orders still bear the name "extraordinary relief." Whenever the plaintiff seeks equitable remedies, the court may apply the doctrines of laches, estoppel, unconscionability, unclean hands, or election of remedies.

(A) Laches and Estoppel

Laches bars a suitor in equity who has not acted promptly in bringing the action. It is reflected in the maxim: "Equity aids the vigilant, not those who slumber on their rights." The doctrine serves to promote diligence on the part of the claimant in asserting rights, to prevent the enforcement of stale claims, and to provide an end to conflict and uncertainty that may surround a dispute. The Supreme Court articulated the fundamental premise of laches in a case over a hundred years ago:

> The doctrine of laches is based upon grounds of public policy, which requires for the peace of society the discouragement of stale demands. And where the difficulty of doing entire justice by reason of the death of the principal witness or witnesses, or from the original transactions having become obscured by time, is attributable to gross negligence or deliberate delay, a court of equity will not aid a party whose application is thus destitute of conscience, good faith and reasonable diligence. Mackall v. Casilear (S.Ct.1890).

The defense of laches has two basic requirements: (1) the claimant had an unreasonable delay in asserting rights, and (2) the delay would operate to unduly prejudice the defendant. There are no mechanical rules for proof of these elements because each case turns on its individual facts, unlike the statute of limitations. Under the Federal Rules of Civil Procedure § 8(c), laches is an affirmative defense; thus, the burden of proving it belongs to the defendant.

The delay necessary for laches is not determined simply by the passage of time. Rather, the defense requires delay that was both unreasonable and prejudicial to the defendant. Laches may apply even if an applicable statute of limitations has not yet run. Thus, a plaintiff who is barred only by laches is precluded from equitable relief but may still seek legal remedies. For example, a plaintiff who is denied specific performance because of laches may still seek contract damages. Laches can bar a claim for these reasons even when a prejudicial delay was caused by an administrative agency rather than the plaintiff. In *Whitfield v. Anheuser–Busch, Inc.* (8th Cir.1987), for example, a ten year delay of the Equal Employment Opportunity Commission did not bar the complainant's claim under the statute of limitations because it did not start to run until after administrative exhaustion. Nonetheless, the delay barred the individual's claim in equity because the defendant's witnesses no longer recalled the event.

The nature of the prejudice may be economic or affect the ability of the defendant to bring a defense to the equitable claim. For example, due to the passage of time the defendant may no longer have access to evidence, witnesses may be unavailable, property changed, or third party rights affected.

Estoppel similarly involves the element of prejudice to the defendant, but the second element is different than laches. Whereas laches concerns delay, estoppel involves actions inconsistent with the rights the plaintiff now asserts. The classic example is that a plaintiff cannot ask equity for an order to remove a neighbor's fence built over the lot line if the plaintiff stood by and watched the fence construction in full knowledge of the location of the lot line. The plaintiff's silence with knowledge of the

facts is an action inconsistent with the right asserted in court.

The defenses of laches and estoppel operate dif-
ferently when the government is a party because
the sovereign is not completely equivalent to a
private party. The government is charged with responsibility for serving the public interest, so courts
give considerable deference to shield it from equitable claims asserted by private parties. Even where it
has waived sovereign immunity the government can
more easily show prejudice to itself when it is
asserting an equitable defense. For the same reason, the sovereign as a plaintiff could not be es-
topped historically, and modern cases have made
only some modifications to this principle.

(B) Unclean Hands

Unclean hands and unconscionability are called
"conscience defenses" because they operate to bar
relief to plaintiffs whose claims are morally tainted
in some way. The foundation of these defenses is
that it is beneath the dignity of the court to grant
equitable relief to unworthy suitors. It does not
matter if the claims are legally sound, and there is
no requirement that the defendant be prejudiced in
any way. Unlike laches and estoppel, these defenses
are premised upon preserving the integrity of the
court and the interest of the public rather than
relative fairness between the parties.

The unclean hands defense gives the court discretion to deny equitable relief to a claimant where
that party has been responsible for some serious

misconduct with respect to the same transaction forming the basis upon which relief is sought. The unclean hands defense is reflected in the maxim, "He who comes into a court of equity must come with clean hands." It means that the plaintiff must not have behaved inequitably with respect to the rights being asserted in the case.

The unclean hands defense may be raised as an affirmative defense in the pleadings or the court may raise it *sua sponte*. When the plaintiff is barred from equity by unclean hands, it is still permissible to bring the claim for damages at law. Only the equitable claim is affected.

The nature of the misconduct that bars equitable relief must be serious but it does not need to rise to the level of fraud or other actionable wrong. Moreover, the taint must be specifically related to the matter before the court and not collateral. It is often said that "equity does not require its suitors to lead blameless lives." In other words, it is only the plaintiff's moral posture with respect to the matter before the court that is at issue and any questionable behavior concerning unrelated matters is not relevant.

(C) Unconscionability

Unconscionability is closely related to unclean hands, but it has distinct characteristics. The doctrine of unconscionability has roots both in law and equity and is embraced both under common law and the Uniform Commercial Code. See Restatement

(Second) of Contracts § 208; U.C.C. § 2–302. The defense is limited specifically to contract remedies.

The determination of unconscionability is made by the court as a matter of law at the time the contract is made. Because the term "unconscionability" itself is not defined under the Code, courts have considerable flexibility in applying the doctrine to limit or exclude contract terms that are considered too oppressive or one-sided. If the court finds that the contract or specific terms amount to unconscionability, there are three options: (1) invalidate the entire agreement, (2) enforce the remainder of the contract without the offending clause, or (3) limit the application of the terms to avoid an unconscionable result. The determination of unconscionability is purely defensive in character as it does not amount to breach of contract nor give rise to a cause of action for damages. Unconscionability is distinguishable from illegality or fraud, which necessarily invalidate the entire contract. A judge who applies the unconscionability defense, either as an equitable defense or under the statutory authority of the U.C.C., is acting in a supervisory role to preserve the integrity of agreements while protecting against unscrupulous practices.

The doctrine of unconscionability involves consideration of both substantive and procedural factors. The substantive issue focuses on whether the bargain reflects "unreasonably favorable terms". A basic illustration would be where a substantial difference exists in the consideration exchanged for the nature of the product or services rendered. For example, in *Jones v. Star Credit Corp.* (N.Y.1969) the court found that a contract where welfare recipients agreed to purchase a freezer for $900 that had a retail value of just $300 was unconscionable. Although courts do not inquire into the adequacy of consideration for purposes of contract formation, an excessive disparity may indicate that the contract is unconscionable. The evaluation of unconscionability is made at the time of contract formation. Therefore, subsequent changes in market conditions that may make a contract bargain unfavorable to one party do not affect the issue of unconscionability.

Terms also may be considered substantively unconscionable by reference to custom or standard practices in the industry. The U.C.C. allows consideration of the commercial setting and the purpose and effect of the contract to aid the court in making its determination regarding unconscionability. See § 2–302(2). The lack of readily available alternatives, such as the inability to obtain housing, goods or services, may also indicate unconscionability. A significant risk of default by the economically weaker party, however, may justify contract terms that reflect the higher degree of risk assumed by the party with stronger bargaining position.

The procedural issue regarding unconscionability is often characterized by the "lack of meaningful choice" by the party with lesser bargaining strength. Although even gross inequality in bargaining power alone does not necessarily make a contract procedurally defective, it may influence a court to scrutinize the manner of formation closely to ensure appropriate appreciation of the risks involved. Contract formation may be suspect in situations where the contract contains fine print or is the product of sharp practices.

The lack of meaningful appreciation of risk undermines the basic assumption of mutual assent in contract law. Therefore, if the court determines that one party would not have entered into the contract had they understood the risks, the contract may be held unconscionable. The Restatement (Second) of Contracts § 208 comment b explains the standard as a contract that "no man in his senses and not under delusion would make and no honest and fair man would accept." The U.C.C. expresses the principle that the doctrine serves to prevent "oppression and unfair surprise". See section 2–302 comment 1. Courts also consider whether the economically stronger and more sophisticated party took advantage of the lack of understanding by the other party.

The most famous unconscionability case at common law is *Campbell Soup Co. v. Wentz* (3d Cir. 1948), where the court refused to enforce a contract between a major soup producer and a farmer because it contained overreaching terms. Campbell Soup entered into a contract with the defendant farmer Wentz to purchase at thirty dollars a ton all the carrots produced on a certain acreage. The contract provided that Wentz had to sell all the carrots to Campbell, but that Campbell was not obligated to purchase them. Furthermore, if Campbell did not want the carrots, Wentz could not sell them to anyone else without permission. This one-sided arrangement reflected the vastly superior bargaining power of Campbell.

The price of carrots subsequently rose to ninety dollars per ton and Wentz violated the contract by selling them on the open market rather than to Campbell at the lower contract price. Campbell needed the carrots and was forced to cover on the open market–possibly purchasing Wentz's contract carrots indirectly at the much higher prices in the open market where Wentz took them.

Campbell sought specific performance of the contract on the grounds that the unique quality of these Chantenay red cored carrots made them particularly suitable for use in vegetable soup. Wentz successfully defended with unconscionability because the court found that the contract was so one-sided as to be unenforceable in equity. Notably, the entire contract was unenforceable even though the unconscionable part of the contract was invoked.

NOT

(D) Election of Remedies

The doctrine of election of remedies provides that when an injured party has two available but inconsistent remedies to redress a harm, the act of choosing one constitutes a binding election that forecloses the other. A classic illustration of the doctrine is that a defrauded party must choose or "elect" between disaffirming the contract through rescission or affirming the contract and seeking damages. The rule developed historically to promote traditional equitable principles against double recovery and undue prejudice of a defendant. Although the policy justifications for the doctrine appear sound, some courts have applied the rule rigidly and produced unexpected and occasional harsh results. The doctrine may operate to extinguish a substantive cause of action even prior to filing suit and under circumstances where the plaintiff never intended to make a true election of remedy.

For example, assume that fraud occurs in a transaction to purchase an automobile. The buyer returns the car to the dealer. The election of remedies doctrine may effectively hold that the buyer has now "elected" to disaffirm the contract, thus precluding an action for damages. Conversely, if the buyer had sent a letter to the dealer demanding damages, the doctrine may deem that conduct an affirmance. In either situation, the buyer may be bound by their initial action even if the dealer has not been prejudiced and no double recovery has occurred. Further, the election may be considered irrevocable even before a suit has been filed and before the aggrieved buyer has sought legal advice.

The rule has come under sharp criticism for its potential for harsh results and historical basis in formalism rather than substance. Rather than following a literal application of the rule, some courts consider whether double recovery in fact would occur or use principles of estoppel, merger or res judicata to analyze the claimant's actions.

The Restatement (Second) of Contracts approaches the issue of election among remedies from the perspective of estoppel. Section 378 provides that the manifestation of a choice of inconsistent remedies does not bar another remedy unless the other party "materially changes his position in reliance on the manifestation." A change of position is considered "material" if allowance of a switch in remedies would be "unjust." See comment a, § 378.

Further, according to the Restatement, the potential for preclusion only occurs where the remedies in fact exist and they are inconsistent with one another. For example, a party cannot obtain specific performance of a contract affirming the bargain and also seek damages for total breach of contract. Some remedies are complementary, however, and serve different purposes because they address different protectable interests in the bargain. Thus, a party may be able to receive restitution and damages in some instances in order to be made whole.

The Uniform Commercial Code specifically rejects the doctrine of election of remedies as a "fundamental policy." U.C.C. § 2–703 Comment 1. Instead, Code remedies are deemed cumulative in nature and include all of the available remedies for breach. Whether the pursuit of one remedy bars another depends on the facts of each individual case rather than on formalistic or mechanical rules. The U.C.C. remedies are to be "liberally administered." 2–711 comment 3. A clear illustration of the more liberal approach of the Code is reflected in section 2–721 regarding remedies for fraud. That provision states that rescission of a contract of sale, nor a rejection or return of goods, bars nor is considered "inconsistent" with a damages claim or any other remedy.

Chapter 6

PRELIMINARY INJUNCTIONS AND TEMPORARY RE-STRAINING ORDERS

Temporary restraining orders and preliminary injunctions are equitable orders available in special circumstances when a plaintiff needs immediate court action to avoid irreversible losses while waiting for the trial on the merits. They are forms of interlocutory relief, which by definition is expedited relief for a short term that a court may give before final adjudication of a case on the merits. The focus of this chapter is on the federal rules related to these remedies. Federal Rule of Civil Procedure 65 governs preliminary injunctions and temporary restraining orders in federal courts, and many states have identical or similar rules but other states vary slightly in the names, procedures, and requirements for preliminary injunctions.

These injunctions are considered "extraordinary" relief that require a strong showing of its necessity. The principal concern underlying issuance of a temporary restraining order is that immediate and irreparable harm will occur during the interim period before the dispute between the parties can be resolved at a full trial on the merits. The interlocutory injunction may issue to prevent commission of an act which threatens injury to the plaintiff's interests respecting the subject of the action or which will render the judgment ineffectual. For example, a court may issue a restraining order to prevent a defendant from removing or disposing of property with an intent to defraud creditors.

A plaintiff must be prepared to compensate a wrongfully enjoined defendant for losses caused by the expedited order regardless of the plaintiff's good faith in seeking it. Unless the plaintiff is ultimately victorious in the underlying case, the plaintiff will be liable for the defendant's proven losses associated with the interlocutory order. Courts generally are reluctant to act when there has not been time for careful deliberation of the full facts of a case.

A common characterization of the purpose of interlocutory injunctions is "to preserve the status quo" until a hearing on the merits can be held. The "status quo" may be characterized as the last actual peaceable uncontested status of the parties to the controversy. It does not alter the legal relations of the parties but instead serves to maintain their relationship for the duration of the order. The status quo can be active or passive. For instance, it can be a condition of action, such as ordering the defendant to continue supplying goods pursuant to a distributorship agreement. An illustration of a passive order would be restraining a developer from razing a building pending resolution of a dispute regarding whether the structure qualified for preservation as a historical landmark under a statute.

The speed of acquisition and the duration of the orders are the primary differences between temporary restraining orders and preliminary injunctions. A temporary restraining order (TRO) is a stop-gap measure for a truly urgent situation to preserve the status quo long enough for a preliminary injunction hearing. After a court has had time to hold a hearing, the TRO will be dissolved if not justified, or replaced with a preliminary injunction to continue holding the status quo until the full trial on the merits of the claim.

Although states are free to adopt procedures that differ from the federal rules covered here, the Supreme Court held in *Carroll v. President and Commissioners of Princess Anne* (S.Ct.1968) that there are Constitutional limits on the issuance of an *ex parte* TRO under state law, at least when First Amendment rights are at stake. In this case speakers belonging to an extremist organization held a rally which included racially provocative remarks. Town officials obtained an *ex parte* TRO to prohibit a second rally because they feared an explosive confrontation. The Supreme Court found that the TRO was procedurally defective because the officials had failed to attempt to give notice to the defendants of the proceedings. The Court explained that when First Amendment rights are at stake, it is particularly important to have all parties present to assure the order is fashioned as narrowly as possible to protect all interests.

(A) Preliminary Injunctions

FRCP 65(a) addresses preliminary injunctions. It provides:

(1) Notice. No preliminary injunction shall be issued without notice to the adverse party.

(2) Consolidation of hearing with trial on merits. Before or after the commencement of the hearing of an application for a preliminary injunction, the court may order the trial of the action on the merits to be advanced and consolidated with the hearing of the application. * * *

Noticeably absent from these provisions are any substantive requirements. Therefore, federal courts have interpreted Rule 65 to incorporate common law substantive requirements traditionally governing equitable orders. Most circuits follow the traditional test for a preliminary injunction. That test has four prerequisites for issuance of a preliminary injunction. They are: (1) a probability of prevailing on the merits; (2) an irreparable injury if the relief is delayed; (3) a balance of hardships favoring the plaintiff, and (4) a showing that the injunction would not be adverse to the public interest. The burden of proof on each of these four elements rests with the movant.

Although the federal Courts of Appeal differ in their approach, they all have in common that plaintiffs must make some showing of the irreparable harm that will result without the order, as well as some showing of the strength of the claim in the underlying suit. The rules differ on whether the plaintiff must always show a "probability" of success on the merits of the underlying claim, or whether a lesser standard is appropriate when the degree of potential harm without the order is especially great.

The application of these requirements is illustrated in a case involving a patient who wanted his health insurance to cover a liver transplant. In *DiDomenico v. Employers Coop. Ind. Trust* (N.D.Ind.1987) the plaintiff sought a preliminary injunction to keep the defendant health insurer from denying coverage for the procedure. The health plan specifically excluded "experimental" liver transplants but the plaintiff's doctors testified at the hearing that adult liver transplants recently had become accepted and were no longer considered experimental by the medical community. The operation was medically necessary to save the patient's life and he could not afford it without the insurance coverage. The district court found that the plaintiff had satisfied each of the traditional requirements for issuance of a preliminary injunction. The most difficult element was irreparable harm because the problem essentially involved a monetary issue. The plaintiff needed to prove that he could not get the operation to save his life in the absence of insurance coverage and that he could not wait to get relief until the end of a full trial on the merits, which might be several years in the future. He succeeded in doing so.

A few federal circuits follow the "alternative test", which allows a plaintiff the choice of establishing the four traditional factors or of satisfying a sliding scale test. The alternative test requires the plaintiff to show "serious questions on the merits" and that the balance of hardships tips decidedly in its favor. The sliding scale operates as follows: the greater the potential irreparability of the harm and the clearer the balance of hardships without the order, the lesser the required showing of strength on the merits of the case. The alternative test, then, may be successfully used where the plaintiff has a relatively weak case on the merits but the potential harm would be extremely serious absent equitable intervention. Conversely, a plaintiff with a strong substantive claim can receive a preliminary injunction with a lesser showing of irreparable harm and balance of hardships, although as a threshold matter there must be irreparable harm. Plaintiffs still bear the burden of proving their case on the merits at trial, but the interlocutory order would give them the opportunity to do so without sustaining the harm.

One early case using this alternative approach provides a good illustration of its application. In *Chalk v. U.S. District Court* (9th Cir.1988) a teacher was reassigned to an administrative position after he was diagnosed with Acquired Immune Deficiency Syndrome (AIDS). He sought a preliminary injunction for reinstatement with a classroom assignment and lost at the district court level. The trial judge found that the teacher suffered no irreparable harm because the administrative position paid the same salary as the classroom assignment. On appeal to the Ninth Circuit, this finding was reversed as clearly erroneous.

The Ninth Circuit in *Chalk* noted that the plaintiff had established a strong likelihood of success on the merits because medical testimony established that there was little risk of his infecting the children with the virus in the classroom setting. Irreparable harm was also present. The appellate court found that the lack of monetary loss was only one aspect of irreparable harm and that the trial court should have focused also on the nature of the alternative work. The plaintiff was a special skills teacher who derived great personal satisfaction from working closely with his small class of hearing-impaired children. In contrast, the reassigned administrative work involved writing grant proposals for which he had no special training nor interest.

The Court of Appeals further addressed the balance of hardships in *Chalk*. The opinion notes that this element is satisfied even though it was unnecessary under the alternative test to find that the balance of hardships favored the plaintiff after the strong showing of success on the merits and irreparable harm. The public expressed fear about the risk of AIDS exposure in schools. The Court of Appeals held that the trial court could retain jurisdiction to remove the teacher from student contact at whatever point qualified medical opinion might determine that his condition poses a risk to the children. For example, if the teacher contracts an opportunistic infection capable of transmission, he can be removed from the classroom. Until then, the preliminary injunction should preserve the *status quo* with the classroom teaching assignment pending the full trial on the merits of the case.

(B) Temporary Restraining Orders

Federal Rule of Civil Procedure 65 contains specific procedural requirements for a temporary restraining orders (TRO). Unlike a preliminary injunction, a TRO may be entered *ex parte,* but only upon a specific showing that immediate and irreparable harm will result before the opposing party could be notified and heard. FRCP 65(b) provides that the order can last only ten days, with a second ten-day extension for good cause or if the other party consents to an extension. In contrast, a preliminary injunction lasts until trial or modification, which means that it could possibly last for years. Even for such a lengthy interlocutory order, the purpose remains the same—to preserve the *status quo*.

The limitations on TROs have been strictly applied by the federal courts. It is an extraordinary remedy to enjoin a party when there has been very little opportunity to receive evidence in the matter. The court must set a time for a preliminary injunction hearing as soon as possible in order to minimize the time of restraint without such a hearing. Further, Rule 52(a) requires the court to state its conclusions of law and findings of fact that constitute the grounds for its action.

Unlike a preliminary injunction, a TRO is not appealable because of its short duration. When the time limitations of Rule 65(b) have been violated, the order "converts" to a preliminary injunction for purposes of appeal. An overextended TRO then gets reversed because it would not be based on a sufficient hearing to support a preliminary injunction. *See* Sims v. Greene (3d Cir.1947).

(C) Injunction Bonds

Federal Rule of Civil Procedure 65(c) provides for security to be provided by the applicant before a court issues a TRO or preliminary injunction. The security required by FRCP 65(c) can be either a bond or guarantee from the defendant. A court may dispense with the posting of a bond if the party seeking injunctive relief has sufficient assets to assure its ability to pay damages, such as when the defendant is a solvent corporation.

The provision of FRCP 65(c) is broad: "No restraining order or preliminary injunction shall issue except upon the giving of security by the applicant, in such sum as the court deems proper, for the payment of such costs and damages as may be incurred or suffered by any party who is found to have been wrongfully enjoined or restrained. * * *." A few courts have interpreted this language to be jurisdictional, but most have interpreted the rule to require that the judge to make a decision on the propriety of a bond and not to ignore a demand entirely. Moreover, although the trial judge has substantial discretion in settling the amount of the bond, it is reversible error to refuse a bond unless there is no risk of monetary loss.

The purpose of requiring a claimant to post bond or provide security is to provide redress for wrongfully enjoined defendants. The bond assures that the defendant will be compensated for any losses occasioned by the order in the event that the plaintiff does not ultimately prevail in the underlying case. The funds in the bond will therefore indemnify the party enjoined from actual, provable damages directly resulting from a wrongfully issued injunction.

Since interlocutory injunctions are issued based on a liberalized showing of probable rights and probable harms, the defendant may sustain losses caused by the injunction and may later prevail in a trial on the merits. The bond operates as a fairness tool to secure payment for those losses incurred during the interim period. The bond provides a convenient repository of funds against which the wrongfully enjoined party can collect actual damages such that the enjoined party does not have to run the risk that the plaintiff is judgment-proof.

Because the claimant must incur costs in posting the bond, this requirement also serves as a check on the zealousness of plaintiffs in instituting litigation. The bond requirement indirectly preserves the dignity of the court and reflects the hesitation of our judicial system to permit orders without time for the judge to hear all the evidence and to reflect on the just result. It is necessary for judges to act in haste in circumstances justifying the grant of a TRO because of the greater danger of injustice without it. Therefore, the function of the security requirement is to guarantee that plaintiffs will compensate defendants for losses caused by that hasty decision. It functions as an exception to the general rule that litigation losses and expenses are borne by the parties themselves.

The court has discretion in setting the amount of a bond, but the enjoined party may request that it be increased in order to more fully protect its interests during the interim period of the interlocutory order. The amount of the bond is generally regarded as a ceiling on the measure of damages potentially recoverable by the restrained party unless the bond was an "open" one or unless security was given without a limitation to recovery. Some courts recognize an exception whereby a claimant may obtain damages in excess of the bond against the plaintiff in "exceptional" cases where the injunction was secured by fraud or malice. The surety always has limited liability.

If the enjoined party subsequently prevails on the merits at trial, the presumption favors some recovery of damages against the bond. The enjoined party must still bear the burden of proving actual losses suffered as a result of the wrongfully issued injunction. Compensable losses include measurable harms caused specifically by the wrongful order, not including distress and humiliation. Losses are not presumed but must be proven with specificity. The bond does not function as a type of forfeiture or liquidated damages, but is restricted to damages caused by the injunction. The standard for recovery is that the injunction was ''wrongfully issued'', but that simply means that the defendant prevailed on the merits, not that bad faith existed.

Chapter 7

CONTEMPT

Equitable orders are enforced by the court's contempt power. A decree in equity, such as an order to pay child support or other injunction, is a personal directive. When a defendant fails to comply with an order, the disobedience is punishable as contempt. Whereas the failure to pay a judgment can result in the court executing against the property of the defendant, a finding of contempt can result in incarceration. The maxim "equity acts in personam" reflects this personal element.

The different types of contempt vary in form and function. There are two basic types of contempt: criminal contempt and civil contempt. The two sub-classifications of criminal contempt are called direct (or summary) and indirect (or constructive). There are also two types of civil contempt: compensatory and coercive. The primary function of criminal contempt is to vindicate the interest of the state in obedience to court orders, whereas the primary function of civil contempt is to benefit the plaintiff for whose benefit the court issued the order.

A disobedient defendant may be held in both criminal and civil contempt for the same act because the functions are different. For example, if a defendant is defiant of an order not to trespass, criminal contempt could punish the defendant for disobedience of the court; civil contempt could compensate the plaintiff for any damage done by the defiant trespass, and/or could coerce the defendant by jail or fine to cease a continuing trespass. This chapter examines these different types and functions of contempt.

(A) Criminal Contempt

There are two categories of criminal contempt, both of which function to vindicate the authority of the court. One type is direct or summary criminal contempt, which operates to maintain order in the courtroom. This contempt is the judge's tool to punish, for example, disruptive courtroom behavior by attorneys, parties, or spectators. It also serves to protect the court's authority by summarily punishing disrespectful behavior that disrupts the orderly administration of the proceedings.

The second type of criminal contempt is called indirect or constructive criminal contempt. It is called "indirect" because it concerns behavior that occurs outside the courtroom. The purpose of indirect contempt is to punish conduct that constitutes an affront to the court when a lawful order is disobeyed. Although the primary function of criminal contempt is the state's interest in the dignity and authority of the court, plaintiffs incidentally benefit as well because the threat of indirect criminal contempt deters defendants from violating the court order designed to benefit the plaintiff.

(1) Indirect Criminal Contempt

Indirect or constructive criminal contempt serves to protect the integrity of the court by ensuring respect for and obedience of its orders. The requirements for indirect contempt are: (1) a valid order issued by a court of competent jurisdiction enjoining the defendant to act or refrain from acting in a certain manner; (2) the defendant had notice of the specific terms of the order; (3) the defendant had the ability to comply with the order; and (4) the defendant intentionally or wilfully disobeyed the order without justifiable excuse. An insolvent defendant, for example, will not be held in criminal contempt for the failure to make scheduled child support payments. However, the defendant cannot wilfully refuse to seek reasonable employment and then claim inability to meet court ordered payments.

Failure to obey a lawful court order is punishable through contempt as a crime. The Supreme Court held in *Bloom v. Illinois* (S.Ct.1968) that criminal contempt is a "crime in the ordinary sense." The Court has further explained that "criminal penalties may not be imposed on someone who has not been afforded the protections that the Constitution requires of such criminal proceedings." Hicks v. Feiock (S.Ct.1988). Those safeguards include the privilege against self-incrimination, the right to a jury trial, the right to proof beyond a reasonable doubt and the right to present a defense. Other rights that apply include double jeopardy, notice of charges, assistance of counsel, and summary process. These Constitutional protections for defendants accused of criminal contempt apply only to disobedience of a court's order outside the presence of the court. Contempts that occur in the court's presence may be immediately adjudged and sanctioned summarily.

The criminal nature of contempt reflects the governmental interest in the obedience of court orders. This interest is so great that the Supreme Court has held that defendants can be punished for contempt even if the order they disobeyed is unconstitutional. In *Walker v. City of Birmingham* (S.Ct. 1967) the Court upheld a contempt sanction against civil rights workers who refused to obey a state court order enjoining a demonstration for racial equality on the city streets. The defendants were not permitted to attack the order collaterally once they disobeyed it; it was their duty to seek a dissolution of the order or to appeal it rather than disobey it. A key fact in that case was that the defendants had a couple of days to act within the state judicial system between the time they received the order and the announced date of the demonstration. Rather than doing so, they held a press conference and announced their intent to defy the court.

The Supreme Court held that such disobedience is punishable with criminal contempt. Even if the court's order was not sustainable, the duty of the defendants was to obey the order or seek its dissolution. The Court explained the policy justifying imposition of criminal contempt as reflecting "a belief that in the fair administration of justice no man can be judge in his own case, however exalted his station, however righteous his motives, and irrespective of his race, color, politics or religion." The Court noted that this was not a situation where the petitioners had attempted to seek dissolution and were met with frustration and delay. Nor was this a case where the order lacked any pretense to validity or was "transparently invalid." The opinion suggests that only those conditions would release the defendants from the duty to obey a court order.

A finding of criminal contempt is not sustainable, however, unless the contemnor is a party bound by the order. The contempt power is premised upon the disobedience of a binding court order, F.R.Civ.P. 65(d) provides that an injunction is "binding only upon the parties to the action, their officers, agents, servants, employees, and attorneys, and upon those persons in active concert or participation with them who receive actual notice of the order by personal service or otherwise." The Supreme Court interpreted this rule in *Regal Knitwear Co. v. NLRB* (S.Ct.1945) to include not only party defendants but those in "privity" with them, at least to the extent that they are in "active concert" with the defendants.

(2) Summary Criminal Contempt

Court may exercise their discretion in limited circumstances to issue a summary or direct contempt sanction in order to maintain proper decorum in the courtroom. Judges are generally hesitant to wield this power because it consolidates all the traditional functions of judge, jury and prosecutor and reposes them in a single person. Therefore, the use of this power is generally reserved for "exceptional circumstances" that significantly interfere with the ability to conduct proceedings in an orderly manner. A summary contempt order reflects a departure from the general rules pertaining to criminal contempt that provide safeguards of notice and a hearing. Such orders are subject to a standard of review of abuse of discretion.

The authority for federal courts to punish direct contempt is 18 U.S.C. § 401, which gives courts "power to punish by fine or imprisonment, at its discretion, such contempt of its authority, and none other, as (1) Misbehavior of any person in its presence or so near thereto as to obstruct the administration of justice ... " The Supreme Court interpreted section (1) in *Nye v. United States* (S.Ct. 1941) to mean "misbehavior in the vicinity of the court disrupting to quiet and order or actually interrupting the court in the conduct of its business."

Summary contempts are further governed by Federal Rules of Criminal Procedure 42(a). This procedural rule requires that a summary contempt in a federal court must be committed in the actual presence of the court and be seen by the presiding judge. Further, the rule contains the procedural safeguard that the judge must certify what he saw and heard. This rule is strictly interpreted in order to protect the rights of the party sanctioned. The judge must personally witness the offending conduct. Therefore, misconduct occurring near the judge is insufficient, such as a scuffle in the back of the courtroom, an inaudible curse, or a slamming of a book on the table when the judge was not watching. The judge has to be sure what happened because the judge is the sole witness in this criminal action. *See* Matter of Contempt of Greenberg (9th Cir.1988).

State courts derive power from state statutes similar to § 401 or from the inherent power of court. State courts often interpret "presence" more broadly that federal courts. Thus, some states would permit a judge to punish as summary contempt an outburst just outside the courtroom door when the judge was on the bench. Although federal law would not permit the use of summary contempt in that situation, some states would consider it sufficiently proximate to the court to permit the exercise of summary contempt power.

(B) Civil Contempt

There are two types of civil contempt, both of which serve to protect the interests of the plaintiff and only incidentally to protect the dignity of the court. Compensatory civil contempt gives the plaintiff damages for injuries caused by the defendant's violation of a court order designed to protect the plaintiff's interests.

The second type of civil contempt is called coercive civil contempt. It ensures compliance for the benefit of the plaintiff by designating daily fines or imprisonment until the defendant stops disobeying an order.

(1) Compensatory Civil Contempt

Compensatory civil contempt provides compensation to a plaintiff for losses caused by the defendant's disobedience of the court order. This type of contempt functions to give the plaintiff damages for losses specifically caused by the disobedience and may be granted in addition to any criminal penalties for the same conduct. For example, consider the situation where a court orders the defendant to cease use of the plaintiff's trade secrets, but then the defendant continues to do so. Through compensatory civil contempt the plaintiff may recover damages caused by the continued use after the court's order. Damage caused before the injunction is recoverable only as damages for tort, but the losses traceable to conduct in defiance of the court order are recoverable as compensatory civil contempt.

This type of contempt recompenses a party for losses directly resulting from the violation of a court order designed to protect that party's rights. Like tort damages, the purpose of the award is to make the plaintiff whole, and the plaintiff must prove damages with specificity. Unlike tort damages, attorneys' fees and costs are a proper element of recovery. The fees must be limited to the pursuit of the contempt claim, however, and do not apply to the underlying claim that produced the order that the defendant disobeyed.

(2) Coercive Civil Contempt

The primary function of civil contempt is to benefit the plaintiff who received the original equitable order; vindication of the court's authority is a derivative benefit. Coercive civil contempt is a tool to ensure compliance with the order designed to protect the plaintiff's rights. It operates to coerce a resistant defendant through the designation of a daily (or other measure of increment) fines or imprisonment until the defendant stops disobeying an order.

For example, if a parent refuses to disclose the location of a child in order thwart the visitation rights of the other parent, the court may imprison the defendant until the parent discloses the information. The defendant is said to have the "keys to the jail in his or her pocket" because release occurs as soon as there is compliance with the court's order. Similarly, if a defendant refuses to produce a document for litigation despite a court order to do so, the court can coerce compliance by imposing an ongoing fine that accrues until the defendant produces the document. Fines are usually unrelated to the measure of damages suffered by the plaintiff and are paid to the government. A few courts have tailored the fine to daily losses, usually intangible ones, and ordered it paid to the plaintiff.

The Supreme Court has held that the amount of a daily civil contempt fine should be determined by several factors. They include "the character and magnitude of the harm threatened by continued contumacy, and the probable effectiveness of any suggested sanctions in bringing about the result desired." United States v. United Mine Workers (S.Ct.1947).

A contempt is not a coercive civil one unless the contemnor has the capacity to end the on-going sanction by compliance with the order. It is criminal contempt if the court has ordered a determinant penalty, such as a specified number of days in jail or a fixed fine.

The sanction for coercive civil contempt is limited to the period of time when coercion is possible. The reason for this limitation is that if the defendant can no longer purge the offense, then any penalty becomes criminal rather than coercive. For example, if a witness is jailed for refusal to testify at a trial even when granted immunity, the sanction must end when the trial is over. At that point the witness can no longer testify and thus could not purge the contempt.

Another limitation on this type of contempt is that it cannot continue once it becomes clear that the coercive measures will never coerce compliance. In that situation, the contemnor must be released from the sanction because the court's ability to coerce the conduct has been "exhausted." For example, if a spouse elects to spend years in jail rather than reveal the location of an asset in a divorce proceeding, the sanction must end at the point where the court is convinced that the coercion will never work.

The Supreme Court has added another limitation to coercive civil contempt in *United Mine Workers v. Bagwell* (S.Ct.1994). This case involved a labor dispute between the UMW and two coal companies in

Virginia. The union engaged in unlawful strike activities, such as blocking access to facilities, physically threatening employees, and damaging company property. The companies obtained an injunction against the unlawful activities, but the union violated the injunction shortly after its issuance. The judge then announced prospective penalties for future violations: $100,000 for violent ones and $20,000 for nonviolent ones. By the end of the strike, the court had found 400 violations of the order by the end of the strike. The cumulative penalties were more than $64 million, of which $12 million went to the companies and $52 million to the state.

The Supreme Court found that in such a circumstance it is necessary to accord criminal safeguards to the defendant. Noting the complexity of the fact-finding and the severity of the penalties, the Court held that Constitutional rights attached even for a civil contempt. The Court left unclear the type of circumstance that triggers this protection and reserved for future cases where to "draw the line" between coercive contempts that do and do not require criminal safeguards. Contempts that involve readily ascertainable acts, such as submission of requested items, are appear unaffected by the decision because *Bagwell* governs only contempts that are complex and severe, but the case leaves open the extent to which coercive civil contempts must be treated as criminal ones. *See* Margit Livingston, *Disobedience and Contempt*, 75 Wash. L. Rev. 345 (2000).

(C) Significance of the Categorization

There are three main reasons for distinguishing between criminal and civil contempt. They are (1) procedural, (2) relation to underlying action, and (3) durability. Judges do not always label a contempt action properly in light of the form and function of the sanction. The court of appeals is not bound by the characterization of the trial court and may overturn a finding of contempt when it does not comport with the standards of its true character. For example, the appellate court may find that a contempt action labeled "civil" is criminal in its function.

(1) Procedural Differences

The differences between procedure and constitutional safeguards for contempt are consistent with the differences between civil and criminal litigation in general. Criminal contempt requires different procedural and constitutional safeguards than civil contempt. Thus, if a trial judge labels a contempt as civil, but it is criminal in its character and purpose, then the trial court's failure to follow the greater requirements of a criminal contempt will cause its reversal on appeal. A criminal contempt cannot be sustained unless criminal procedure was used. *See* In re Stewart (5th Cir.1978).

(2) Relation to Underlying Action

Criminal contempt is a separate offense, independent from the underlying case that produced the order violated by the defendant. It is a crime in the ordinary sense. As such, it is immediately appealable. In contrast, civil contempt is tied to the underlying case and must be appealed at the same time as that case.

(3) Durability

Criminal contempt is a separate offense, independent from the underlying case that produced the order violated by the defendant. Therefore, it survives without regard to the success of the underlying case that produced the order that the defendant violated. Consider, for example, that a court orders a defendant ex-employee not to use a customer list taken from the former employer. The defendant violates the order and is held in criminal contempt. On appeal of the employer's action, the court holds that the employer does not have a protectable interest in this customer list and therefore the ex-employee wins the case. The finding of contempt still stands, however, because it was criminal contempt.

In contrast, civil contempt sanctions depend upon the plaintiff's ultimate success on the merits in the underlying case. Thus, in the customer list example, if the court had ordered the defendant to pay compensation for use of the list, that order would fall when the employer lost the case.

The Supreme Court established this principle as an alternative ground to its holding in *United States v. United Mine Workers* (S.Ct.1947). The issue in that case was whether a union could strike against the employer when the United States had taken over the coal mines under its emergency powers during World War II. The United States wanted an injunction against the strike, but the union invoked the Norris–LaGuardia Act that prohibits federal courts from enjoining labor strikes. The United States countered that it was not an "employer" within the meaning of the Act. The federal district court issued an injunction against the union to forbid a strike while the court considered a statutory coverage issue. The union struck in violation of the order and was held in criminal contempt. The Supreme Court found in favor of the plaintiff on the coverage issue, but held as an alternative ground that the defendant could be punished criminally for violating the court's order regardless of whether the plaintiff prevailed in the underlying action. Distinguishing between civil and criminal contempt, the Court held that the difference in the function of the two contempts justifies the difference in their durability.

Chapter 8

STRUCTURAL, RESTORATIVE, AND PROPHYLACTIC INJUNCTIONS

(A) Modern Forms and Functions of Injunctions

There are four types of injunctions: preventive, structural, restorative, and prophylactic. The preventive injunction was the subject of Chapter 3. Whereas the preventive injunction has deep roots in the common law, the last three have been conceived and recognized as independent varieties of injunctions over the past half century.

The purpose of the preventive injunction is to prevent the defendant from inflicting future injury on the plaintiff. Preventive injunctions can be prohibitory or mandatory in character, but each still focuses on abating or ameliorating prospective harms in some fashion. As examined in Chapter 3, to receive a preventive injunction the plaintiff must prove the violation of a legally protected interest, the inadequacy of legal remedies, the imminent likelihood of sustaining irreparable harm absent equitable intervention, and the balance of hardships favoring the grant of equitable relief. The court also considers public interest, if applicable, as well as its own interest in the ability to fashion and supervise the order. The court may issue an interlocutory injunction, such as a preliminary injunction, to preserve the status quo pending a trial on the merits. Finally, a court may issue a permanent injunction that affects the legal relationship of the parties until subsequently modified or dissolved. The other three types of injunctions share these requirements but differ in their forms and functions.

The labels for types of injunctions—preventive, structural, restorative, and prophylactic—are not typically used in opinions themselves. They are used to describe the form and function of each injunction. The labels are useful in order to understand the nature of what the court has done and to fit it within a framework of similar cases.

(B) Structural Injunctions

The name of structural injunctions reflects the fact that courts in certain cases have undertaken supervision over institutional policies and practices where Constitutional violations exist in those institutions. Structural injunctions are a modern phenomenon born of necessity from developments in Constitutional law where the Supreme Court has identified substantive rights whose enforcement requires substantial judicial supervision. These rights concern the treatment of individuals by institutions, such as the right not to suffer inhumane treatment in a prison or public mental hospital. Enforcement of such rights by injunction has become an implicit part of the Constitutional guarantee of protecting individual liberties from inappropriate government action.

The beginning of structural injunctions was with school desegregation cases following the Supreme Court's second decision in *Brown v. Board of Education* (S.Ct.1955). In the first *Brown* decision in 1954 the Court decided the principle that racially segregated school violated the guarantee of equal protection. The second decision in 1955 addressed the remedial issue of how to correct violations of this right. The Court explained that

> courts may consider problems related to administration, arising from the physical condition of the school plant, the school transportation system, personnel, revision of school districts and attendance areas into compact units to achieve a system of determining admission to the public schools on a nonracial basis, and revision of local laws and regulations which may be necessary in solving the foregoing problems. They will also consider the adequacy of any plans the defendants may propose to meet these problems and to effectuate a transition to a racially nondiscriminatory school system. During this period of transition, the courts will retain jurisdiction of these cases.

In the years that followed, federal district courts retained jurisdiction in school desegregation cases and worked through the administrative changes necessary in integrating schools. Each of the items mentioned in the Supreme Court's list in the quoted material was litigated extensively. The utility of injunctions "structured" to address the nature of the Constitutional infirmities is twofold: the order can be written with specificity to correct particular problems and the court retains jurisdiction to supervise compliance with its orders.

In cases involving Constitutional violations at the institutional level, defendants are first ordered to submit plans to cure the offensive conditions. When defendants do not respond cooperatively or quickly, then judges often undertake to mandate particular changes. Structural injunctions typically involve long and costly battles that frustrate class plaintiffs, defendants, and judges. The importance of the rights that they vindicate justifies the cost and attendant difficulties and frustrations. Structural injunctions reflect the traditional province of equity jurisdiction to exercise discretion to balance hardships and to consider public interest in protecting important Constitutional rights.

(C) Restorative Injunctions

A restorative injunction, also called a reparative injunction, functions to correct the present by undoing the effects of a past wrong. The notion of "restoring" means that it focuses retroactively and not just prospectively, as does the traditional preventive injunction. For example, a tainted election process affects future governance; the wrong can only be corrected by turning back time, in some sense, and redoing the election. An early example of this type or injunction was Bell v. Southwell (5th Cir.1967), where the court found that a racially tainted election could only be cured by another election.

A reinstatement order in an employment discrimination case is another form of restorative injunction. It returns the plaintiff to the position held before the wrong. In Vasquez v. Bannworths, Inc. (Tex.1986), for example, a farm worker was fired for complaining to the United Farm Workers union about the lack of clean water and sanitary toilet facilities in the fields, as required by law. The trial court issued a preventive injunction which ordered the defendant not to discriminate against her further in the event she ever worked for the defendant again. This future-oriented injunction had no practical effect when she had already been fired and was unlikely to be rehired voluntarily. The appellate court found that a restorative injunction was necessary—namely, an order that the plaintiff be rehired and thus restored to the position held before the wrong.

(D) Prophylactic Injunctions

A prophylactic injunction shares the goal of a preventive injunction to prevent future harm to the plaintiff, but it seeks to safeguard the plaintiff's rights by ordering behavior that is not otherwise required by law. Whereas a preventive injunction prohibits future or ongoing behavior that violates rights, such as prohibiting a repeating or continuing trespass, a prophylactic injunction concerns behavior indirectly related to those rights. For example, a prophylactic injunction related to trespass would require a trucking company to inform its employees about the boundary of the parking lot. Although a company's failure to communicate with employees is not a wrong in itself, the goal of such an injunction would be to prevent the defendant's employees from continuing to park on the neighboring lot of the plaintiff.

Thus, the approach of a prophylactic injunction is to direct the defendant's behavior so as to minimize the chance that wrongs might recur in the future. In one famous case, Bundy v. Jackson (D.C.Cir. 1981), an employer maintained a work force where the social atmosphere encouraged and perpetuated sexual harassment so pervasively that it violated federal law. Judge Skelly Wright's opinion held that the trial court should order the employer to take specific steps not otherwise required by law, such as educating the employees on their responsibility not to harass co-workers. The lack of such education is not in itself a violation of federal law in the absence of a court order. The court ordered the measures only because it deemed that future infractions of the plaintiffs' rights were likely without extra protections.

Chapter 9

SPECIAL ISSUES IN EQUITY

(A) Statutory Limitations on Discretion

A basic principle of equity is the court's wide discretion to grant or withhold relief based upon balancing the equities and hardships of the parties and consideration of the public interest. An injunction is not considered an automatic right, even in situations where the claimant demonstrates a right deserving of legal redress. Although a court possesses subject matter jurisdiction over a dispute, the essence of equitable jurisdiction is that the judge retains discretion as to the propriety of granting or denying relief. *See* United States v. Oakland Cannabis Buyers' Cooperative (S.Ct.2001).

When a claim is brought under a statute, the court looks to the statutory provision for remedies. If no remedies are enumerated, common law remedies may be implied. Where a statute is silent with respect to equitable relief but expressly provides for damages, the court must determine whether equitable remedies should be implied. Conversely, when a statute provides for only equitable remedies, the issue is whether damages should be implied. The process of statutory interpretation begins with legislative intent, which may be gleaned from legislative history and the plain language of the statute. In some cases, the statutory enumeration of particular remedies and the omission of others have led courts to find a negative implication that only the remedies expressed were intended by the legislature and all others excluded. In some other cases, when courts have been confronted with an absence of clear guidance from the text or history of a statute, judges have invoked the general policy behind the statute to allow additional remedies.

Claimants seeking an injunction with respect specific conduct, such as environmental injuries, find statutes a helpful supplement to the common law for several reasons. The court may find that the legislature has already balanced public and private interests when proscribing specified conduct. Further, the showings of inadequate remedy at law and irreparable harm may be liberalized by the presence of the statute depending upon how the court interprets legislative intent. Although the presence of a statute may make it somewhat easier to obtain a prohibitory injunction than at common law, courts still maintain their equitable discretion to issue or withhold relief and also with respect to how an injunction may be tailored. Claimants still must meet the common law requirements for injunctive relief: an inadequate remedy at law, irreparable harm, balance of hardships favoring the injunction, and public interest in enjoining the imminent harm threatened. The claimant must show that the right asserted fits within the scope of the statutory scheme and that they are within the class of per-

sons sought to be protected by the statute. A gener-
alized interest in advancing the public interest is
insufficient.

The Supreme Court strongly endorsed the principle of equitable discretion in the provision of statutory remedies in *Hecht Co. v. Bowles* (S.Ct.1944).
The case involved price controls during World War
II under the Emergency Price Control Act of 1942.
The governmental Administrator argued that he
was automatically entitled to an injunction upon
showing a violation of the Act. Although a company
had violated certain provisions of the Act, it had
demonstrated its substantial good faith efforts in
attempted compliance with it. The Administrator
nevertheless contended that the statutory language
"shall be granted" required courts to issue an injunction automatically upon a showing of any violation. The Supreme Court rejected that argument,
finding room for discretion under the statute to
select other remedies that may be more appropriate.
Under these facts, trial court held that an injunction would be ineffective and not in the public
interest. The Court found that it unlikely that
Congress intended a drastic departure from the
traditions of equity by removing discretion from the
trial judge. Justice Douglas' opinion for the Court
observed: "The historic injunctive process was designed to deter, not to punish. The essence of equity
jurisdiction has been the power of the Chancellor to
do equity and to mold each decree to the necessities
of the particular case. Flexibility rather than rigidity have distinguished it."

There are nonetheless a few statutes that have been interpreted as removing the equitable discretion of the courts, either by a statutory preclusion of an injunction or by a statutory mandate of one. In either instance, the legislative intent must clearly guide courts in their remedial options.

The most famous example of this category of statute is the Court's interpretation of the Endangered Species Act of 1973 in *Tennessee Valley Authority v. Hill* (S.Ct.1978). The Court determined that the Act required the trial court to enjoin the continued construction of a federal dam project once it determined that a species was protected by the Act and that the project threatened its habitat. The species in question was a snail darter, which was technically covered by the definition of endangered species under the Act. The Court held that the absolute language of the Act removed all discretion from the trial court to balance the relative importance of this species with the economic significance of the federal project which Congress had explicitly funded and which was near completion at the time the snail darter was discovered. The Court reasoned that the language, history and structure of the Act demonstrated the clear Congressional intent that protection of certain species should be given the highest of priorities because their value was "incalculable." The Court further found that because Congress had already considered the public interest and expressed its intent favoring protection of endangered species, the doctrine of separation of

powers precluded traditional judicial balancing of
equities and withdrew its discretion.

Whereas *TVA v. Hill* illustrates the statutory
mandate of an injunction, a few other statutes are
interpreted specifically to prohibit injunctions. One
example is Internal Revenue Code § 7421(a), which
effectively prohibits injunctions against the Internal
Revenue Service from collecting taxes. Another illustration is the Norris–LaGuardia Act, 29 U.S.C.
§ 104 which prevents federal courts from enjoining
labor disputes by removing federal "jurisdiction"
over such issues. On the state level, some jurisdictions have limited anti-injunction statutes where
public interest strongly disfavors interference with
the operations of certain local industries. For example, some heavily agricultural states have anti-injunction legislation barring issuance of injunctions
against normal farming activities. The provisions
are often contained within nuisance statutes that
allow for the recovery of damages where a farming
activity substantially interferes with an adjoining
landowner.

(B) Enjoining Speech

Courts are extremely hesitant to issue injunctions
to restrain free speech and freedom of the press.
The judicial disinclination of prior restraint corresponds to the strong democratic notion favoring the
robust exchange of ideas in the marketplace. *See*
New York Times v. Sullivan (S.Ct.1964). Consequently, a strong presumption exists against prior
restraint of speech and a heavy burden of proof is

required to justify issuance of an injunction. *See* Organization for a Better Austin v. Keefe (S.Ct. 1971). When freedom of speech is exercised in a way that seriously interferes with other important rights, a court may restrain it with a narrowly tailored order.

An early expression of the strong judicial deference given to freedom of the press was shown in *Near v. Minnesota* (S.Ct.1931). The Court invalidated a state statute that provided for abatement as a public nuisance any "malicious, scandalous and defamatory" newspaper article concerning political and public figures. The Court acknowledged that freedom of the press is not an absolute right and the state can punish abuses. The dangers associated with censorship, however, were considered greater than potential sanctions or subsequent punishment. The Court recognized the liberty of the press historically, "the chief purpose of the guaranty to prevent previous restraints upon publication. The struggle in England, directed against the legislative power of the licenser, resulted in renunciation of the censorship of the press."

The freedom of the press must be balanced, in some instances, with other constitutional protections. For instance, in *Nebraska Press Assoc. v. Stuart* (S.Ct.1976) the Court invalidated a pre-trial restraining order issued by a state court prohibiting news media from disseminating information about a criminal trial. The Court acknowledged the conflict between the Sixth Amendment right to a fair trial and the First Amendment guarantee of freedom of the press. However, the Court found that the barriers to prior restraint remained high and the presumption against its use invalidated the injunction. The Court reasoned that the burden of showing a "clear and present danger" that pre-trial publicity could impinge upon the defendant's right to a fair trial had not been met.

Not all injunctions that burden speech are necessarily subject to the prior restraint doctrine requiring close judicial scrutiny. For example, in *Madsen v. Women's Health Center, Inc.* (S.Ct.1994), an order imposing noise and distance limitations on anti-abortion protesters was deemed content-neutral because it focused on proscribing certain conduct. Although the persons subject to the order may have shared a common viewpoint, the burden on speech was considered only incidental to the conduct prohibited. The Court recognized that injunctions carry a greater risk of censorship and discriminatory application than ordinances, but noted that they have the advantage of being specifically tailored to afford more precise relief than a statute. The judicial role in evaluating injunctions affecting conduct in a public forum, then, must be to "burden no more speech than is necessary" to serve a significant governmental interest.

Similarly, in *Shenck v. Pro–Choice Network of Western N.Y.* (S.Ct.1997), the Court upheld the constitutionality of an injunction establishing a "fixed buffer zone" prohibiting protestors from interfering with patients and counselors within 15 feet of an abortion clinic, but found that further provisions that imposed "floating buffer zones" burdened more speech than was necessary.

The judicial hesitancy to enjoin free expression applies even in situations potentially implicating national security. In the leading case, *New York Times v. United States* (S.Ct.1971) the Court invalidated a lower court restraint on publication by newspapers of a classified study dealing with Vietnam War policies of the United States. The Court found that, absent statutory directive, the government failed to meet its heavy burden of justification for use of prior restraint.

(C) Enjoining Litigation

A court sitting in equity will generally decline to issue injunctions that restrict access to civil courts or to interfere with the operation of the criminal justice system. A strong public policy favors open access to courts. The policy is supported by the American Rule that each party bears its own litigation expenses, absent showing of bad faith, contract, or a fee-shifting statute. Therefore, the instances in which a court may exercise its discretion to prohibit filing of an action are reserved for the exceptional cases.

One situation in which a court may be persuaded to issue a prohibitory injunction is where a pattern emerges that the claimant is abusing the judicial system by filing repetitive, frivolous, and sometimes vexatious claims. If such a finding is made, the court would potentially issue an injunction for two reasons. The first justification would be to protect the party seeking equitable relief from expending valuable time and resources in being forced to defend against such actions. Second, the court would be protecting the judicial system itself from being overburdened with handling meritless cases. The party seeking equitable relief has a heavy burden to demonstrate that litigation rises to the level of harassment or excessiveness.

Any prohibitory injunction involves a measure of future prediction that the conduct proscribed is threatened and imminently likely to occur absent equitable intervention. That future prediction, of course, is particularly difficult where only a single case has been filed and the opposing party may not institute litigation again.

Where a court issues an injunction against filing civil suits, care must be taken to write the order with sufficient clarity and specificity that the party enjoined understands the scope of the subject matter of the order. A violation of the order would potentially subject the party restrained to an order of contempt.

Injunctions against criminal prosecutions are extremely rare. Historically, courts commonly expressed the view that, absent statutory authorization, an equity court had no "jurisdiction" over the prosecution, punishment or pardon of crimes and misdemeanors. *See* In re Sawyer (S.Ct.1888). The modern view, however, firmly holds that courts with general equity powers do possess the power to restrain criminal prosecutions but should exercise their discretion cautiously and reserve such orders for exceptional cases.

The policy reasons supporting a general rule of non-intervention focus on the respective purposes and functions of the civil and criminal courts. Courts of equity are not constituted nor designed to deal with criminal proceedings, lack power to punish persons who violate penal statutes, and do not compensate persons injured as a consequence of criminal statutes.

The exceptional circumstances in which a court may enjoin criminal proceedings, then, generally require (1) a clear showing that an injunction is necessary to adequately safeguard important rights of the accused, (2) the remedy at law of defending under the relevant criminal statute is inadequate, and (3) that the order can be imposed without imposing an undue burden upon or show disrespect to the criminal court.

An illustration of where a state civil court may enjoin a threatened or existing criminal case in its jurisdiction is upon a demonstration of improper prosecutorial motivation. An extra-territorial injunction seeking to restrain a criminal prosecution in another state would have the additional problem of impracticality of enforcement against non-resident parties.

Principles of federalism further limit the willingness of a federal court to issue an injunction against state court proceedings. The strong policy of judicial restraint reflects respect for the integrity of the state court system. The court, as a general policy, will find that a party has an adequate remedy at law by defending themselves in the criminal cases.

(D) Enjoining Nuisances

Nuisance law presents certain unique challenges to courts with respect to determining the propriety of injunctive relief. The nature of nuisance law involves a comparative evaluation of competing land uses. The balancing process occurs on two separate levels. First, the threshold requirements to maintain an action are that the defendant's conduct constitutes a substantial and unreasonable interference with the use and enjoyment of the plaintiff's property or public interests. Not every interference with other land uses will amount to an actionable nuisance, but it must be unreasonable based upon consideration of the benefits of the activity, suitability to the locale, and the gravity of the harm. Once the standards for entitlement are met, the court will also consider if the threatened harm is immediate, the injury constitutes irreparable harm, no adequate remedy at law exists, and the balance of hardships favors equitable intervention. The court will determine the extent to which damages will sufficiently redress the injury and the relevance of public interest factors.

Unless an activity is proscribed by statute and constitutes a nuisance *per se*, the court will determine if the conduct constitutes an unreasonable and substantial interference with the use and enjoyment of another's land. See Restatement (Second) of Torts § 821D. Even if the conduct violates a statute, however, the court will still consider whether damages or injunctive relief would be the more effective remedy.

Consider the situation where a large factory is discharging effluent into a drainage ditch and the waste leaches into an aquifer, resulting in the contamination of crops being raised on adjacent land. The surrounding landowners may successfully bring a claim for private nuisance and collect temporary damages, such as diminished rental value or lost crops for the past invasion of their land. The periodic payment of damages, though, would probably not substantially affect the operations of the factory in the future.

The court would balance the economic and public interest advantages associated with operation of the factory, such as providing jobs and taxes, with the health and safety impact on the landowners. The concern with awarding damages rather than injunctive relief is that the it would effectively be licensing a continuing wrong and allow payment of damages as a type of private eminent domain. Since the activity is of an ongoing nature, however, the court may find that damages are not an adequate and effective remedy because the pollution will remain unabated and the landowners would be forced to bring multiple suits for compensation. Further, if the interference is particularly hazardous to human health or the environment, such as polluting with toxic waste, the court may likely issue an injunction to abate the activity. In any event, injunctions against a nuisance are never granted automatically nor a matter of right, but the decision rests with the sound discretion of the judge sitting in equity.

An illustration of the difficulties in balancing disparate interests such as economics with health and safety may be found in the famous case, *Boomer v. Atlantic Cement Company* (N.Y.1970). In Boomer, neighboring landowners sought to enjoin the operation of a large cement plant, claiming that the dirt, smoke and vibrations emanating from the plant constituted a nuisance. The court granted an injunction but conditioned its effect on the defendant's payment of permanent damages to compensate for the economic losses to their property. The court considered the social and economic repercussions from shutting down the factory in terms of lost jobs and taxes, balanced with the problems posed by the cement dust. The court, in favoring a legal remedy, expressed deference to the legislature as being in a better position to balance the various public and private interests at stake by promulgating a comprehensive solution to the issues of air pollution.

A zoning ordinance may affect the availability and the nature of injunctive relief. The defendant's compliance with state or local governmental regulations is relevant to the assessment of the reasonableness of the activity and its suitability to the locale. Compliance with all pertinent regulations is not always sufficient to defeat an injunction, however. If a court finds an activity to present an imminent and extremely hazardous danger to public health and safety, an injunction would be issued in the public interest to foreclose the threat.

Some jurisdictions have passed anti-injunction acts affecting nuisance cases. The statutes generally preclude courts from restraining business activities that are being reasonably conducted in compliance with zoning regulations. An anti-injunction act does not necessarily end the court's equitable jurisdiction, but may affect the manner in which it exercises discretion.

An injunction case always involves some degree of future prediction. The judge must determine both the likelihood and degree of future threatened harm absent the injunction. If the claimant seeks an injunction against an activity that has already occurred, relief will be denied following the maxim that "equity will not enjoin a completed act." An illustration is where a factory malfunction causes noxious gases to escape and damage an orchard located on adjacent land. The factory subsequently repairs the problem and no further incidents occur. A court will not issue an injunction on the basis that the incident is not reasonably imminent to occur; therefore, such an order would be without merit. On the other hand, where an ongoing activity presents a continuous invasion of an important interest an injunction may be proper because the remedy at law is inadequate.

A court is faced with an especially difficult task of prediction when the activity sought to be enjoined is causing no current harm and poses only an uncertain future threat. An injunction is not justified if its basis is solely that a tort may possibly occur. For example, in *Nicholson v. Connecticut Half–Way House, Inc.* (Conn.1966), residents sought to enjoin the prospective use of defendant's property as a temporary residence for selected parolees from state prison. The plaintiffs claimed that the parolees might commit criminal acts in their neighborhood and that the half-way house would cause their property values to depreciate. The court denied injunctive relief because unsubstantiated fears could not justify the intervention of equity.

Another issue involving the role of equity in nuisance law deals with reconciling the timing of priority of location of competing land uses. Under the "coming to the nuisance" doctrine, courts historically denied equitable relief to a party who knowingly located adjacent to an existing, lawfully conducted business and then complained that the land use constituted a nuisance. The rationale behind foreclosing equitable relief was that the party either impliedly consented to the offending use or should have reasonably foreseen that the activity would cause a significant interference with their own property interests. Further, the doctrine gives some measure of protection to justifiable investment expectations of the existing land uses. The general rule of shielding the existing use from equitable action has been losing force in modern law, however.

An early example of the changing trend may be seen in the notable decision, *Spur Industries, Inc. v.*

Del E. Webb Development Co. (Ariz.1972). A major residential development situated outside a metropolitan area slowly expanded such that a number of houses were in close proximity to a large cattle feedlot. The noxious odors emanating from the feedlot interfered with the residents and potential buyers, leading the developer to seek an injunction against the operation as a public and private nuisance. The court granted the injunction and mandated the relocation of the feedlot but conditioned the order upon the developer's indemnification of expenses for the move. Although the feedlot had priority in time over the residential development, the court found that it did not automatically foreclose equitable relief. The court was persuaded that the public interest favored enjoining the feedlot based upon the magnitude of the interference and the inadequate remedy at law.

(E) Enjoining Crimes

In some situations the same conduct may potentially implicate both civil and criminal laws. A common illustration is where certain actions may constitute a public nuisance, which is proscribed under both civil and criminal statutes. If so, and a claimant seeks an injunction through civil courts to abate the offending behavior, the judge sitting in equity faces a dilemma whether or not to exercise jurisdiction.

The general rule historically is reflected by the maxim that "equity will not enjoin a crime." The statement itself is somewhat overbroad, however.

The civil court certainly retains power to enjoin but often will defer to enforcement of the violation through the criminal justice system.

Several important reasons support such deference. First, if the civil court issued an injunction, the defendant would lose the right to jury trial in an equity proceeding. Second, the standard of proof for issuance of an equitable order is lower than beyond a reasonable doubt under the criminal statutes. Third, the judge may determine that an adequate remedy at law exists in the penal sanctions available through enforcement of the criminal statutes. Finally, the equity court may refrain from acting out of deference and respect to the criminal courts and, in the interests of judicial economy, to avoid duplicative proceedings.

The general notion of restraint embodied in the rule is not followed in all cases, however. If the enforcement of the criminal laws does not appear to be effective to abate the conduct, then an equity court may decide that a civil injunction would be an appropriate remedy. An example would be where operation of a gambling house violates provisions of a state or local statute, but the only penalty specified for violation under the statutory scheme is a small fine. Several actions of enforcement of the statute have resulted in imposition of fines but the gambling house continues in operation. At that juncture, the equity court may determine that the criminal statute does not constitute an adequate legal remedy to address the proscribed conduct and may issue a permanent injunction.

For example, in *Goose v. Commonwealth* (Ky. 1947), the court issued an injunction against the proprietors of a gambling establishment. The court found that numerous arrests of the operators during a five year period had not been effective in abating the criminal conduct. The state therefore had no adequate remedy at law, and the ongoing activities caused irreparable harm to the public. The court stated: "The ground of the jurisdiction is the ability of the chancellor to give a more complete and perfect remedy by a perpetual injunction. It is a weapon from the arsenal of equity to be used to protect Society—to meet the social need that continuation of the offenses at a given place shall be repressed."

The outer limit of the intervention of equity courts may be seen in another well known case, *State v. Red Owl Stores* (Minn.1958). The state requested an injunction to restrain the defendant corporations from selling and distributing certain drugs without obtaining the necessary registration and licenses required by the state's Pharmacy Act. The trial court had denied the injunctive relief on the grounds that the exclusive remedy in the Act was enforcement by criminal prosecution. The Minnesota Supreme Court reversed, however, on the basis that the state lacked an adequate remedy at law to enforce a public health measure. The legal remedy was inadequate because enforcement through the sanctions in the Act would require a multiplicity of actions, even though the state had not yet instituted any enforcement action of the criminal statute.

Rather than a blanket rule of restraint, then, a more accurate statement of the modern approach is that equity courts will generally decline to exercise jurisdiction where a criminal statute offers a sanction against the conduct at issue. Thus, while equity will certainly not enjoin conduct merely because it also violates a criminal statute, neither is a court entirely precluded from such action. The critical determinant is whether or not the injunction will serve a useful purpose and not inappropriately deprive the accused of important safeguards otherwise available through the criminal justice system.

Chapter 10

BREACH OF CONTRACT REMEDIES

A. Common Law Contract Damages

(1) Expectancy

Traditional contract law recognizes and protects the injured party's expectancy, reliance, and restitutionary interests in the bargain. The basic purpose of compensatory damages under both the common law and the Uniform Commercial Code is to place the injured party in as good a position as if full performance had been rendered under the contract. The measure of recovery will vary depending upon which of the interests are asserted, although in some instances a breach may give rise to recovery under more than one of the three interests. Additional policy considerations that are sometimes reflected in the law of contract damages are avoiding economic waste, promoting efficient breach of contract to move goods and services to the highest bidder, and advancing the public interest. Since an award of damages for breach of contract does not require judicial supervision or enforcement in the same manner as equitable decrees, the oversight role of the court is not generally emphasized in determining entitlement and measurement of compensation.

(2) Reliance

The non-breaching party may seek damages for expenses incurred in reliance upon performance of contractual duties. Sometimes reliance damages may be the only relief sought, such as where the plaintiff cannot prove expectancy damages with reasonable certainty. For example, if someone has entered into a losing contract and has no expectancy damages, that party may still recover expenses incurred in reliance upon the performance of duties prior to the contract breach. In other situations, expenses incurred in reliance upon the performance of contractual duties may be added to the loss of expectancy.

(3) Restitution

Restitution is the third interest protected under contract law. Confusion sometimes occurs, however, in distinguishing between restitution as an entire field of law that may independently provide remedies from the interest reflected within a bargained-for exchange. The law of restitution has a lengthy heritage both at law and in equity, emerging in the dual system of law courts and Chancery courts that developed through the influence of the church in England. Although some of the forms and requirements varied between the two lines of restitution, they shared the common purpose of preventing unjust enrichment. The basic premise of restitution was to serve the ends of justice by properly "restoring" back to the rightful party benefits that were held unjustly by the defendant. Wrongdoing was not a requirement for disgorging the benefit, as restitution could properly be used to restore funds mistakenly paid to the wrong party. On the equity side, some of the restitutionary remedies included constructive trusts, equitable liens, accounting for profits, subrogation, and cancellation and reformation of instruments. On the law side, the remedies emerged in the form of "common counts", such as "money had and received", "quantum valebant", and "quantum meruit". These were generally called "quasi-contracts" because the court would order a payment of money for either goods or services based on a fictional construct, not an actual contract. The remedy was unrelated to an express contract or implied-in-fact contract, but instead was a contract implied-in-law to achieve the result of preventing unjust enrichment.

Completely apart from these formal remedial devices at law and equity, the law also recognized and protected the restitutionary *interest* that was embodied within an express contract. This interest served the same basic function of restoring back to the injured party some benefit that should not be retained by the other contracting party. Consider the following illustration: Buyer pays the full contract price of $10,000 to purchase 1,000 widgets from Seller, but Seller only delivers 800 widgets. The Buyer now has the right to enter the market and purchase substitute widgets to replace the shortfall of 200 widgets and will receive the difference between the contract and market price for the goods. As an additional item of damages, the $2,000 overpayment for non-delivered goods should be repaid to protect Buyer's restitutionary interest in the contract. The restitutionary interest in this example would be combined with protecting the Buyer's expectancy interest.

(4) General and Special Damages

The common law of contracts classifies damages as either "general" or "special". The importance of distinguishing between them turns on the principle of foreseeability, which found early expression in the English case, *Hadley v. Baxendale* (Ex.Ct.1854):

Where two parties have made a contract which one of them had broken, the damages which the other party ought to receive in respect of such breach of contract should be such as may fairly and reasonably be considered either arising naturally, *i.e.*, according to the usual course of things, from such breach of contract itself, or such as may reasonably be supposed to have been in the contemplation of both parties, at the time they made the contract, as the probable result of the breach of it.

Thus, general damages are those which flow directly and immediately as a natural consequence of the kind of wrongful act by the breaching party. The law conclusively presumes such damages to be foreseen or contemplated by the defendant. In contrast, special damages do not always follow from the kind of conduct involved. Accordingly, breaching parties are liable only where the evidence shows that they should have reasonably foreseen the kind of harm resulting from their non-performance at the time of entering the agreement. A common illustration of the distinction involves a construction contract with defects in performance. The repairs to correct the defective condition would be classified as general damages and do not require special foreseeability. On the other hand, if the owner sought lost profits due to delays in opening a restaurant because of the faulty construction, those damages would be "special" and necessitate foreseeability by the contractor.

Although the terms "general" and "special" damages have diminished in application in some jurisdictions, the essence of the special damages criteria has been embraced by the Uniform Commercial Code § 2–715(2) with respect to the availability of consequential damages to an aggrieved buyer of goods and under § 2–708(2) of lost profits for sellers. Section 2–715(2) determines recoverability of damages depending upon whether the seller, at the time of contracting, had "reason to know" of general or particular requirements of the buyer. General damages are reflected in § 2–714 as providing recovery for the difference in the value of accepted but non-conforming goods compared to the value as warranted.

(5) Cost Rule and Value Rule

The common law recognizes two competing measures of damages for loss of the expectancy interest, generally called the "cost rule" and the "value rule." A typical scenario in which these rules may come into effect would involve incomplete or defective construction under a building contract. The cost rule would allow the non-breaching party to recover the damages to complete or remedy the defective condition to conform to the contract. The value rule would measure damages by the diminution in value of the performance received compared to the value as promised.

The difficulty arises where remedying the defective condition may involve expenditures that would substantially exceed the diminution in value measure. Although theoretically both measures of damages would provide recovery for the expectancy interest, most courts will award the diminution in value where the cost of repairs would be clearly disproportionate to the value to the injured party of correcting the defect.

The policy supporting that result often is stated as avoidance of economic waste that may accrue from making excessively costly repairs. Other courts point to concerns of giving a windfall to the non-breaching party for the cost to repair. The windfall argument recognizes that the injured party may simply choose to retain the damages awarded and forego making the repairs.

For example, in the leading case of *Jacob & Youngs v. Kent* (N.Y.1921), a contractor built a residence, but installed a brand of plumbing pipe which differed from the specifications. The mistake was made in good faith and was discovered only after completion of the project. The court held that the proper measure of damages would be the difference in value between the pipe specified and the type actually installed, reasoning that it would be economically wasteful to tear down the house just to obtain the small benefit of substituting a different brand of pipe.

A few courts have awarded damages for the higher cost to complete performance on the basis that the defendant breached the contract willfully or acted in bad faith. *See* Groves v. John Wunder Co. (Minn.1939). The vast majority of courts, though, have focused on the degree of proportionality between the two measures of damages as the controlling factor rather than on the subjective motivation for the contract breach.

(6) New Business Rule

Courts have traditionally held that new businesses cannot recover lost profits for breach of contract. The rationale for precluding recovery is that the lack of sufficient operating history for new businesses necessarily makes prospective profits too speculative, contingent, and remote to satisfy the legal standard of reasonable certainty. The distinction drawn between new business ventures and existing operations for awards of future profits became so common that some courts elevated it to virtually a *per se* rule.

A growing trend, however, focuses on whether the damages can be established with sufficient evidence rather than preclude recovery automatically. These courts acknowledge that a new business faces a greater burden of proof in establishing the loss of anticipated profits but allow the claimant an opportunity to produce evidence to meet the reasonable certainty standard. Two possible methods have been recognized to prove lost profits. Under the "before and after" theory, plaintiffs introduce evidence of their track record of profits prior to and following the breach of contract. An alternative method, called the "yardstick" test, considers evidence of profits by comparable business operations. The Restatement (Second) of Contracts § 352 comment b takes a more neutral position and provides that the difficulty of proving lost profits should vary depending upon the nature of the transaction.

(7) Liquidated Damages

Parties to a contract may decide to "liquidate" or specify the amount of damages that would be payable to the non-breaching party in the event of a material breach of contract. The use of a liquidated damages clause may offer several advantages, such as allowing the parties to control or limit their economic risk, to curtail the uncertainties associated with proving actual damages, and to avoid the time and expense of litigation. Additionally, the clauses promote judicial economy through reduced litigation and burden on the court system. On the other hand, some critics express concern that private parties should not supplant the role of courts in styling their own remedy, that the potential for excessive damages could deter efficient breach of contract, and that a liquidated damages clause could be the product of unfairness or overreaching in the bargaining process. The balance often drawn is to use a liquidated damages clause in agreements where, at the time of contract formation, the parties anticipate difficulties could exist in proving actual compensatory damages and decide to make a reasoned forecast of losses if a breach occurred. For example, such clauses are used with some frequency in construction contracts, employment agreements, and real estate transactions.

Although parties possess considerable discretion in stipulating in advance an amount of damages, they are still limited by basic principles otherwise governing compensatory damages. Consequently, a liquidated damages provision will be upheld when it meets the standard of a good faith, reasonable pre-estimate of actual damages. In that sense, the clause simply serves as substitutionary measure for performance in the event of a breach. In contrast, in situations where a court determines that the purpose of the clause is to compel performance or to punish non-performance with excessive damages, it will be considered a penalty and thus unenforceable on grounds of public policy. The *in terrorem* effect of an onerous liquidated damages clause transcends the goal of compensation and is viewed in the same judicial light as unconscionable bargains. An unreasonably low stipulated damages for breach of contract may also reflect overreaching by the favored party.

The labels applied by the parties to characterize a provision as an enforceable liquidated damages clause rather than a penalty are not controlling. Although some courts may assign some weight to the terminology selected by the parties as one factor in interpreting the validity of a liquidated damages clause, most jurisdictions look beyond the intent to the substance and function for determining enforceability.

The law of liquidated damages is consistent with the common law policy of allowing efficient contract breach. In that sense, a contracting party should be permitted to pay the liquidated amount as a type of compensatory damages resulting from a breach in exchange for the opportunity to shift goods or services to a different source in order to maximize economic resources. In contrast, a clause that essentially functions to punish or deter a contract breach would be inefficient in economic terms and contradict the principle of fair compensation.

The traditional test to evaluate the validity of a liquidated damages provision is whether, at the time the parties entered the contract, the stipulated amount bears a reasonable relationship to the anticipated or actual losses caused by a breach, and damages are difficult to determine. See Uniform Commercial Code § 2–718(1) and Restatement (Second) of Contracts § 356(1). The U.C.C. adds the factor of "inconvenience or non-feasibility" of otherwise obtaining an adequate remedy as another consideration in evaluating reasonableness.

The reasonableness of a liquidated damages clause may be shown by evaluating either the antic-

ipated or actual harm from the breach. Since the
parties are dealing with various uncertainties of
future risks and potential losses at the time of
contracting, subsequent proof of actual harm attributable to the breach invariably with be either higher or lower than the specified amount. Because the
amount of provable actual damages will almost certainly vary from that stipulated in the contract, the
inquiry of reasonableness in estimation is predicated upon the factors objectively contemplated by the
parties at the time of contract formation. The very
uncertainty in predicting future harm militates
against requiring an exact correlation of actual to
liquidated damages. For example, if parties to an
employment contract include a liquidated damages
clause, they may do so in recognition that a discharge of the employee by the corporation in breach
of the agreement may cause the employee certain
subjective injuries like harm to reputation, that
would be difficult to prove or calculate. Similarly, a
new business venture may choose to include a liquidated damages clause in a construction contract
because any future lost profits from delays in construction would potentially be speculative. As long
as the parties have a reasonable basis for the selection of the amount, such as by reference to market
conditions, custom in the industry, prior dealings,
or other risk factors, the clause will typically be
upheld under principles of freedom of contract. The
measure of damages under a liquidated clause is
basically an "all or nothing" proposition, as the

court will decide whether or not the provision satisfies the standard of reasonableness.

Another aspect to the traditional common law
test for upholding a liquidated damages clause is
that the potential damages which might accrue as a
result of a breach must be uncertain and difficult to
ascertain. The Restatement (Second) of Contracts
§ 356 comment b approaches the uncertainty of loss
factor with a flexible test based on the nature of the
harm. So, to the extent that the nature of the
transaction would involve a high degree of difficulty
in proving actual losses, more discretion may be
given to the amount selected by the parties. The
Uniform Commercial Code test in § 2–718(1) has
reduced difficulty of loss from being treated as a
separate factor to serving as one consideration regarding the reasonableness of the clause.

If a liquidated damages clause is deemed invalid,
the non-breaching party may still seek to prove
actual compensatory damages resulting from the
breach. The standard requirements of proving cau-
sation, entitlement, and measurement of compensatory damages would apply.

Several issues exist with respect to whether a
liquidated damages clause is considered the exclusive remedy for breach of contract or just an alternative course of action. The prevailing view is that,
unless the contract states otherwise, the non-
breaching party may choose whether to rely upon
the liquidated sum or seek other remedies at law or
equity. Another perspective is that the provision as

the sole option available. In the context of equity, the liquidated damages clause becomes the focus for the inquiry whether the damages constituted an adequate remedy at law. In any event, double recovery of the liquidated amount and compensatory damages is precluded by ordinary principles of contract damages.

In summary, the law of liquidated damages reflects a tension between conflicting goals. It is socially desirable for parties to fix damages in the event of breach when the amount bears a reasonable proportion to the probable loss and the actual loss is difficult to estimate with precision. Such a provision, however, should not have the effect of deterring breach through compulsion because of the potential high economic loss.

(B) Sale of Goods Contracts

(1) Buyers' Remedies

The damages remedies with respect to contracts for the sale of goods are governed by Article 2 of the Uniform Commercial Code. The remedies available to non-breaching buyers essentially correspond to those available to non-breaching sellers. The buyer's expectancy interest is compensated with three principal elements of damages: (1) contract-market differential damages; (2) incidental losses incurred as a result of the breach; and (3) consequential losses that are reasonably foreseeable by the breaching party, including items such as lost profits.

Further, Article 2 provides buyers and sellers with corresponding remedies of rescission and restitution [U.C.C. §§ 2–702, 2–711] and specific performance or an action for the price See U.C.C. §§ 2–716 and 2–709. The remedies are considered cumulatively available to the non-breaching party, as the U.C.C. rejects the election of remedies doctrine "as a fundamental policy." U.C.C. § 2–703, comment 1. In keeping with the general policy of the liberal administration of remedies, the Code requires that damages be proven with reasonable certainty rather than mathematical exactitude. See comment 1 to U.C.C. § 1–106.

(a) Cover

One of the primary remedies available to a non-breaching buyer under the Code is the allowance of "cover" damages for purchasing goods in the market to replace those due under the contract. Following a breach, an aggrieved buyer may enter the market and make a reasonable purchase of substitute goods. See U.C.C. § 2–712. The measure of damages is the difference between the cost to cover and the contract price plus incidental or consequential damages, less expenses saved. The requirements for effecting cover are that the buyer must (1) act in good faith, (2) without unreasonable delay, and (3) make a reasonable purchase of substitute goods. The buyer, in effecting cover, does not have to replicate exactly the terms of the original contract. The acquired goods must be "reasonable" substitutes, even if not identical to those due under the contract. Further, the buyer may buy in a single contract or a series and may vary credit and delivery terms. The guiding principle is that the buyer must act in a commercially reasonable manner.

The concept of cover achieves several purposes. The affirmative grant of authority to enter the market and obtain needed goods protects the expectancy interest and business needs of the buyer. The seller is also protected in that the buyer is precluded from claiming any consequential damages which could have been reasonably avoided by cover. See U.C.C. § 2–715. In essence, a commercially reasonable transaction effecting cover provides evidence of the market for the goods.

The buyer has no duty or obligation to cover, however, but may choose to resort to other remedies for the breach. The Code effectively provides the same basic formula for calculating damages under the alternative provision, section 2–713, as would be used if the buyer actually entered the market and obtained substitute goods. That section provides that the measure of damages for non-delivery or repudiation by the seller is the difference between the market price and the contract price at the time the buyer learned of the breach. *See* U.C.C. § 2–713. The same two adjustments to the damages formula are included, as incidental or consequential damages are added and expenses saved are subtracted from the total award.

(b) Consequential Damages

The Code carries forward the common law concept of special damages for lost profits under the classification of "consequential" damages under § 2–715(2). An aggrieved buyer may recover consequential damages by showing (1) that the seller had reason to know of the buyer's general or particular requirements and needs at the time of contracting, and (2) the losses could not have been prevented by cover or otherwise.

The concept of "reason to know" carries forward the common law doctrine of foreseeability, which can be satisfied by either an objective standard of what a reasonable person in the seller's position would know or a subjective test of what the seller actually knew. *See* R.I. Lampus Co. v. Neville Cement Products Corp. (Pa.1977). The Code rejects the restrictive common law "tacit agreement" test that required a buyer to prove that the seller specifically contemplated and consciously assumed the risk of consequential damages. *See* Globe Refining Co. v. Landa Cotton Oil Co. (S.Ct.1903). The buyer must only show that the seller reasonably contemplated that some lost profits would be sustained in the event of a breach, not the exact amount. The evidence to sustain consequential damages includes reference to the particular character, condition, or circumstances of the non-breaching party that were reasonably foreseeable by the seller. The types of evidence that may justify lost profits could include prior history of dealing between the parties, industry custom, and specific language in the contract.

The Code incorporates the doctrine of mitigation to preclude or limit consequential damages that could have been reasonably prevented by cover or otherwise. The buyer must only take reasonable steps to mitigate, however, and is not required to incur substantial expenses or assume excessive risk.

(c) Difference-in-Value Damages

The common law idea of general damages is reflected under section § 2–714 which provides damages for non-conforming goods that are accepted by a buyer. The measure of damages is the difference between the actual value of the goods as received compared to the value as warranted. Unlike consequential damages, damages for non-conforming goods do not require foreseeability but are conclusively presumed based on the nature of the transaction.

(2) Seller's Remedies

Sellers generally have access to the same categories of damages as are available to buyers under the Code, with some differences in nomenclature and application. The Code seeks to balance remedies in an even-handed fashion, so theoretically no particular advantage or disadvantage accrues to either side as a non-breaching party. Each of the basic damages remedies are complemented by the entitlement to incidental damages to reimburse the seller for expenses reasonably incurred as a result of the breach. Any expenses saved as a result of the buyer's breach are subtracted from the total damages awarded.

Although sellers are not entitled to consequential damages, they may recover lost profits and reasonable overhead if the ordinary measure of damages under § 2–708(1) is "inadequate to put the seller in as good a position as performance." *See* U.C.C. § 2–708(2).

(a) Resale Damages

The most basic damages remedy available to sellers is the mirror image of the buyer's right to cover. A seller may enter the market and effect a resale of the contract goods and obtain the difference in the contract price less the resale price, plus incidental damages and less expenses saved. See U.C.C. § 2–706(1). An effective resale provides probative evidence of the market price at the time and place performance should have been rendered by the buyer. Therefore, the resale must be conducted in good faith and in a commercially reasonable manner, either at public or private sale. See U.C.C. § 2–706(2). In the event that proof of relevant market prices at the time of tender is lacking, courts have some flexibility in using a reasonable substitute to make the necessary calculations. *See* U.C.C. § 2–723(2).

If the resale occurs at private sale, the seller must provide reasonable notification to the buyer of the intention to resell. The seller is not accountable for any profits made on the resale. If the seller chooses not to resell the goods, the measure of recovery is the contract price minus the market price at the time and place for tender, with the usual adjustments for costs incurred or saved. Just as a non-breaching buyer is not required to cover, an aggrieved seller is under no obligation to resell goods following a breach. Section 2–708(1) provides a comparable remedy for recovering damages measured by the difference between the market price at the time and place for tender and the contract price, plus incidental damages and less expenses saved.

(b) Lost Profits

One of the most difficult sections of the Code involves the issue of lost profits for sellers under U.C.C. § 2–708(2). That section provides that if the damages for resale-contract price differential is

> inadequate to put the seller in as good a position as performance would have done then the measure of damages is the profit (including reasonable overhead) which the seller would have made from full performance by the buyer, together with any incidental damages * * * due allowance for costs reasonably incurred and due credit for payments or proceeds of resale.

One of the oddities of section 2–708(2) is that it does not use the term "consequential" damages, which is used for buyers seeking lost profits pursuant to § 2–715(2). Nevertheless, sellers may resort to § 2–708(2) for potential lost profits in certain situations.

The predicate to using this provision is a showing that the basic measure of damages for taking the difference between a resale and the contract price is "inadequate." Courts have recognized three situations in which § 2–708(2) may provide an appropriate remedy to a non-breaching seller, two of which are relatively non-controversial. The first involves "jobbers" or "middlemen" who enter contracts to purchase goods in order to resell them to third parties. The jobber never actually obtains possession of the contract goods, so is not in a position to effect a resale into the market. The second situation involves component parts sellers who manufacture or assemble contract goods. Section 2–708(1) does not apply because no finished article exists that may be resold into the market. The most difficult and controversial issue pertains to "lost volume sellers" who seek recovery of lost profits.

Consider the following hypothetical: ABC Corporation enters into a contract to manufacture and sell 1,000 widgets to XYZ, Inc. for $1.00 per unit. Prior to the date due for delivery, XYZ unequivocally repudiates the contract and ABC enters into a second contract to sell the 1,000 widgets on the same terms to a third party. If ABC seeks recovery of damages pursuant to § 2–708(1), the differential between the original contract and the resale price would yield zero damages because the prices for the goods remained the same. Therefore, ABC argues that it has lost the "opportunity" to make two sales, and correspondingly two profits, instead of one. Following that approach, then, ABC would claim that its damages under § 2–708(1) are "inadequate" because they do not adequately reflect compensation for the lost opportunity to make the second profit.

For example, in *Neri v. Retail Marine Corporation* (N.Y.1972), the seller contracted to sell a new boat, which it ordered and received from its supplier. The buyer then repudiated the contract. The seller subsequently sold the boat to another buyer for the same price. The court relied on § 2–708(2) and awarded the seller its lost profits under the original contract. The court reasoned that market damages would be "inadequate" to put the seller in as good a position as performance under the initial contract. The court drew an analogy to an auto dealer with an inexhaustible supply of cars. A breach of an agreement to purchase a car at a standard price would cost that dealer a sale even though a third party may subsequently buy the car at the same price. In other words, had the breaching buyer performed, the seller would have made two sales instead of one. While the seller in *Neri* was a retailer, the lost volume seller rule is also applicable to manufacturers.

The requirements for asserting lost volume seller status generally are: (1) the seller would have solicited the second buyer even if no breach occurred under the first contract, (2) the second buyer would have purchased the contract goods, and (3) the seller had the requisite capacity to perform under both contracts. This theory has been criticized on the grounds that not every breach of contract necessarily produces a loss and resulting damages. Accordingly, giving recovery for lost volume seller status contravenes the basic goal of compensatory damages of placing the non-breaching party in the same position as full performance of the agreement.

(c) Action on the Price

The legal remedy available to non-breaching sellers that roughly corresponds to the equitable remedy of specific performance for buyers is called an action on the price under § 2–709. This remedy is much narrower in scope and application than others available to sellers so is used sparingly. The situations in which an action on the price may be utilized are: (1) where the buyer has accepted goods, (2) conforming goods have been lost or destroyed after risk of loss has passed to the buyer, or (3) goods are identified to the contract and the resale is impracticable. The principal situation in which a seller may seek an action on the price is where no ready market exists in which the seller can effect a commercially reasonable resale, such as where goods have been specially manufactured to meet a buyer's particular needs. In contrast with specific performance, an action on the price is a legal remedy that provides a damages award. It is not an equitable decree and does not bind the party *in personam*.

(C) Land Sale Contracts

Remedies for breach of contract for the sale of land may include either damages or specific performance. The remedy of specific performance has been traditionally available to non-breaching purchasers of land. The rationale for authorizing equitable relief is that every parcel of land is unique, so the remedy at law for damages would be inadequate. Courts retain discretion, however, to determine the propriety of granting specific performance. Therefore, equitable relief may be denied if the balance of hardships weighs heavily in favor of the vendor. Another practical problem affecting specific performance would be where the vendor cannot deliver full title to the property. If the nature of the defect is relatively minor, the court may still order specific performance with an abatement or adjustment to the purchase price. If the defect is major, however, the court may choose not to order a conveyance that is substantially different from the original agreement.

Assuming that specific performance is not granted, non-breaching vendees may seek damages for their expectancy interest. The majority of jurisdictions follow the "American" rule of damages for a vendor's breach which results from a deficiency in title. The rule provides for an award of the benefit of the bargain to a vendee for a vendor's breach of an executory contract to convey title. The general formula for calculating recovery is the difference between the contract price and the fair market value of the land on the date of the breach, plus expenses incurred and reduced by benefits received or expenses saved. The buyer also may be entitled to recover lost profits. The claimant must prove, with reasonable certainty, that such losses were reasonably foreseeable by the seller at the time of the contract. When a sale of land is in gross, or by the tract, the vendor generally will not be liable for a deficiency in acreage absent fraud in the transaction. On the other hand, where the agreement is on a per acre basis, a court will charge the vendor with damages to reflect the deficiency.

A minority of jurisdictions follow the "English" rule which only provides for restitution of amounts paid by the vendee, together with interest and reliance expenses incurred in connection with the agreement. Under the English Rule, the non-breaching vendee cannot recover damages for the loss of expectancy absent a showing of the vendor's bad faith, fraud or deceit. If granted restitution, the purchaser may also receive a lien on the realty to secure recovery of sums previously paid.

In the event of a breach by the vendee, the vendor may seek recovery of the purchase price, as a corollary remedy to specific performance. Otherwise, the vendor may look to recovery of the earnest money as a type of liquidated damages clause. Real estate contracts typically contain earnest money provisions that specify an amount payable to a non-breaching vendor in the event of a material breach by the vendee. Such provisions, irrespective of the label assigned by the parties, are treated as liquidated damages clauses. Therefore, the provision will be upheld if meeting the standard of a good faith, reasonable pre-estimate of actual compensatory damages. In contrast, if the court concludes that the earnest money provision constitutes a "penalty" designed to compel performance and not approximate reasonable compensation, it will be invalidated. Even if the clause is invalidated, however, the non-breaching party may still seek compensatory damages for the loss of benefit of the bargain. The measure of recovery for loss of expectancy is the difference in market price versus contract price at the time of the breach. The amount of damages recoverable through that measure may be less than the sum stipulated in the liquidated damages clause, however. The claimant bears the burden of proving damages with reasonable certainty.

(D) Equitable Remedies

(1) Rescission

In some instances one or both parties to a contract may desire to terminate their future obligations under the agreement. The concept of unmaking or avoiding a contract is called rescission, which may be accomplished at law or in equity. The parties to a bilateral contract that has performance remaining on both sides may mutually agree to discharge or rescind their remaining obligations.

More problematic, of course, is where just one party seeks to rescind. A party may rescind at law by giving notice of the intent to rescind, offer to give restitution of benefits received, and demand restoration of benefits conferred. If the other party complies, restitution is accomplished by agreement. If not, then the contract is deemed rescinded but recovery will depend on appropriate relief through maintaining an action at law. The grounds for rescission may include mistake, fraud, duress, unconscionability, or misrepresentation. Courts will consider the materiality of the grounds for rescission, and will reserve such a drastic remedy for the instances in which the basic assumptions of the contract are affected. An action for rescission operates typically as a complete avoidance of the contract. Partial rescission will not be ordered unless the contract itself is considered divisible and the parties fairly returned to their original position.

An alternative method for obtaining rescission is seeking intervention of a court of equity. A claimant may seek rescission in equity in order to recover specific or unique property. Assuming that the court grants equitable rescission, the property may be conveyed through a restitutionary remedy such as a constructive trust.

(2) Reformation

Reformation is an equitable remedy that may be used to conform an agreement to reflect the true intentions of the parties. In contrast with rescission, reformation does not lead to termination of the contract. Instead, the purpose of reformation is to rectify some inaccuracy in the written terms to make it correspond to the original understanding of the parties. A prime illustration of the need for reformation is where a mutual mistake of a material fact occurs with respect to a description or quantity of the subject matter of the contract. The court may correct any errors that occurred in the integration of the agreement to conform to the parties' reasonable expectations. The parol evidence rule does not bar the admission of extrinsic evidence that may be used solely to explain and correct the terms of the contract for reformation purposes, rather than to vary or contradict its terms.

Chapter 11

TORT DAMAGES

The primary goal of tort damages is compensation to the injured party, although other goals such as efficiency and avoidance of waste influence the calculation of the loss. Another interest in damage law is the promotion of out-of-court settlement; to that end damage law seeks to present predictable and objective measures.

In circumstances where a tension develops between apparently conflicting goals, jurisdictions have sought to achieve damages rules that reflect appropriate compromises. Because there is no perfect way always to reach fair results that are also efficient ones, the law continues to evolve. Different jurisdictions formulate slightly different rules to resolve conflicting interests, and the rules are further subject to exceptions that constantly erode them as the law changes. Tort damage law rules thus can appear arbitrary without an understanding of the unifying principles that govern them and the conflicts in remedial goals that change them. This chapter and the ones that follow address those principles and conflicts.

This chapter covers compensatory damages for tort injuries to personal property, real property, personal injury, and wrongful death/survival actions. These are the most common categories of tort damages. Chapters 12 and 13 then present limitations and adjustments to those damages. Chapter 14 explores two other types of injuries for which damages in tort are only sometimes available because they present special remedial problems: emotional distress without personal injury and economic losses without physical injury. Chapter 15 covering punitive damages is the last chapter on the subject of damages. Punitive damages are unlike compensatory damages because they seek to punish rather than to compensate.

By definition, compensatory damages in tort are designed to make the injured party whole by substituting money for tangible and intangible losses caused by the wrong. In contrast, the chapters after the ones on damages concern restitution, where the goal is to disgorge benefits that are unjust for the defendant to retain. The difference in orientation of these remedies frequently produces different dollar amounts.

(A) Personal Property Damages

Recovery for harm to personal property is divided into two categories: destroyed property and injured property. Personal property, such as an automobile, can be destroyed either through total destruction or through injury whose cost of repair exceeds the value of the chattel. Property that can be repaired at a cost less than its value is considered reparably injured. It is a finding of fact whether the injury is reparable, and legal consequences follow accordingly.

(1) Destroyed Personal Property

The measure for the loss of destroyed personal property is its fair market value immediately before its destruction less any value it has as scrap. Consider, for example, the destruction of a couple's car by a negligent driver in an accident. Their damages will be the fair market value of the car, considering its age and condition, minus any remaining value. The principle behind this measure is that the couple has lost that asset off their personal balance sheet, so that the paper record of their wealth will be restored when they receive the fair market value of the car. The car simply turns into cash and thus the total value of their assets remains the same before and after the accident. It is as if they had sold the car.

Fair market value is the price that a willing buyer and seller would find in an arms' length transaction with each party fully informed. In theory, if the couple wants another car they can take the damages and purchase a used car exactly like the one they lost. In practice, most people find that they cannot replace a lost car with one exactly like it for the same price and, even if they can, there is no compensation for the time and trouble involved in obtaining a replacement. Despite these deficiencies in the law from the plaintiffs' point of view, the advantage of the rule is that fair market value is a predictable number that is easy to ascertain. Because items such as cars are frequently destroyed and because coverage is typically through the insurance of the negligent party, this measure encourages efficient settlement of the numerous claims.

Problems of measurement arise when there is no fair market value for the item destroyed. The most common situation involves "unique" personal property, such as family heirlooms, or where no ascertainable market exists to gather sufficient data to compute damages. In those situations, owners may use other evidence of value, including replacement costs, depreciation, expert opinion and the amount of insurance carried on the item.

When personal property has no real market value, most courts allow the owner to recover the actual value of the property to the owner. The same rule applies when the value of the property to the owner exceeds the market value. The "actual value to the owner" is nonetheless an objective measure and does not include sentimental value.

Sentimental value is generally not allowed for the destruction of personal property. If a tortfeasor negligently breaks a vase that had been a treasured gift from a lost friend, there is no recovery for the emotional attachment to the property. The objective measure of value has the advantage of producing a more easily ascertained value, which is favored for the purpose of promoting settlement, even though the owner is undercompensated for the loss. Courts also fear that permitting damages for the loss of a sentimental item will encourage false claims.

An exception to the rule prohibiting sentimental value is permitted in some jurisdictions. The exception is for items whose primary value is generally recognized as sentimental, such as trophies and wedding rings. *See* Campins v. Capels (Ind.App. 1984). The policy reason for this exception is that there is less chance of falsified claims of emotional attachment for items that are generally sentimental ones.

Another exception to the standard measure of fair market value for damages to personal property is a special rule for clothes and household goods that are personal consumables. Although a person may own used clothes for business purposes, such as the owner of a second-hand shop, most people own used clothes because they consume them. Used clothes do have a fair market value and that measure could be appropriate for their destruction in a fire of second-hand store. For an ordinary consumer, however, an award of fair market value for clothes lost in a house fire would be a hardship. As a practical matter, consumers of goods must replace them rather than simply adjust their balance sheets. Therefore, most jurisdictions permit a "value to the owner" measure for items such as clothes and household goods. The rule does not permit replacement cost, although that cost is a factor in determining the value to the owner. Other factors include the original cost, the quality, and the condition of the property.

(2) Reparable Personal Property

When personal property has been damaged but is capable of repair, the owner is entitled to recover the cost to repair if that cost is economically feasible. When repairs are not economically feasible, the plaintiff can recover only the diminution in the value of the property. The rationale for limiting recovery to diminution in value is to prevent a windfall and avoid economic waste. Consider, for example, that a couple's car is injured by a negligent driver in an accident. They can receive the cost to repair the car unless that cost exceeds its fair market value before the accident. If it does, then they receive only the difference in the fair market value of the car before and after the accident–a measure which is called diminution in value. Some jurisdictions limit repair costs to the diminution in value as well, but most permit full repair costs as long as they do not exceed the value of the property before the accident and they are not grossly disproportionate to the diminution in value of the property.

As a practical matter, the cost of repair and the diminution in value of property by injury are usually very close to the same amount. If a car has a dented fender, for example, its value has diminished by the cost of fixing the fender. There are situations where the measures will be very different, however. The issue of whether to limit recovery for damaged personal property to its diminution in value is well illustrated by the famous case *Hewlett v. Barge Bertie* (4th Cir.1969).

The plaintiff *Hewlett* owned a barge called BA–1401 which was dented by the defendant's vessel, the Barge Bertie. BA–1401 had been in an accident prior to this one at issue and it had not been repaired. It was seaworthy, but it had only limited uses. The dent did not affect the seaworthiness of BA–1401 and no actual damages were shown. The Fourth Circuit overturned the award of nominal damages in admiralty and awarded the cost to repair the barge. Whereas repairs could be made for less than the value of the barge as scrap, the dent did not cause any diminution in the value of the barge. The court held that the cost of repair would be the appropriate measure of recovery unless the cost exceeded the fair market of the barge at the time of the injury. The dissenting judge would have awarded the plaintiff the lesser of the cost to repair or the diminution in value. The opinion notes that the plaintiff suffered no economic loss and that the cost of repairs would be economically infeasible where the cost exceeded the diminution in value.

Many courts recognize an exception to the principle of awarding the lesser of cost to repair or diminution in value where the item has some "special" or "personal" value to the owner. This exception is not intended to indirectly award excessive costs merely for sentimental purposes, but rather acknowledges that some types of personal property may have an objective reason to be repaired. An illustration may be a treasured heirloom quilt that has been damaged by tortious conduct. Even if the cost to restore the quilt to its pre-tort condition may exceed the diminution in value, a court may allow damages for repair to accommodate the interests of the owner. The result would not be seen as a windfall because the owner would likely use the damages award to make the necessary repairs.

Most jurisdictions permit additional damages for the loss of the use of the property while it is being repaired. Thus, the couple could receive compensation for their inability to use the car while it is in the shop. Most jurisdictions do not allow for loss of use damages when property is destroyed and limit such recovery to loss of use during repair. The theory is that the owner of destroyed property is essentially "selling" the property to the tortfeasor because the measure of damages is the fair market price. Continuing that analogy, there is no "loss of use" when one sells property; there is simply a payment of the cash value. Some jurisdictions recognize the modern reality of consumers in our society and permit loss of use damages for a reasonable period of time for replacement of a destroyed item. This more personalized element to the loss, however, reduces the certainty of the calculation and thus reduces the speed and efficiency of settlements.

(B) Real Property Damages

The same themes and policy conflicts that affect damages for injury to personal property appear also in the law of damages for injury to real property. For harm to realty that is reparable, courts generally use two competing measures of damages: cost to restore or diminution in fair market value before and after the harm. Although both measures are intended to compensate the landowner for the losses suffered, the damages actually awarded may vary significantly. Jurisdictions struggle with issues such as whether to award cost of repair damages if they are greater than the overall diminution in value of the property. That question is the counterpart of the one in personal property damages which asks if repair costs can exceed the diminution in value of the chattel.

The Restatement (Second) of Torts § 929 provides that costs of restoration should be ordinarily allowable as the proper measure of damages unless it is "disproportionate" to the diminution in value. Some courts will limit recovery to the lesser of cost to repair or diminution in market value caused by the damage. The reason for limiting damages in such a manner is to avoid economic waste and a windfall to the prevailing party. Some courts allow the higher measure of recovery if the owner has a reason personal to the owner for making the repairs. For example, if the damage occurs to a home that is the owner's residence, a court may allow costs of repairs even if exceeding the diminution in value.

If an injury to real property cannot be repaired, then the award is limited to the diminution in value of the land, which is measured as the difference between the fair market value of the property immediately before the injury and its fair market value immediately after it. The counterpart in personal property damages is the award of fair market value for destruction.

Courts also commonly distinguish between "permanent" and "temporary" injuries to land. One problem that arises, though, is that those terms have no definitive independent meaning. The characterization of the nature and extent of the injury to land as either temporary or permanent is made by considering whether the injury is abatable or reversible and whether it is reasonably susceptible to restoration and repair without undue expense or hardship. There are three significant consequences that result from classification of injury to land as either permanent or temporary: (1) the measure of damages, (2) the applicable statute of limitations, and (3) the availability of equitable relief.

The award of damages for permanent harm to land is the diminution in value of the property, which is measured as the difference in the fair market value of the property immediately before and after the injury. This recovery takes into account past and future diminished productivity of the land. In contrast, the measure of damages for temporary harm is the reasonable cost of restoration or repair of the land to its former condition. Some courts use a fair rental value for the period of the injury to compensate for temporary harms for the loss of use of the land. Since the process of restoration of land may be difficult and costly, many courts limit recovery to not exceed the depreciated value of the land. The rationale for limiting damages to the diminution in value of the realty is to avoid economic waste. Further, the rule of avoidable consequences requires the injured party to diminish the loss as reasonably as possible.

If the wrongful act adversely affected the value or use of the entire parcel, it is appropriate to compute the damages on the basis of the total acreage and not just on the portion damaged. In some cases there may be permanent damage which occurs to one part of a tract while another portion of the parcel suffers injuries causing only temporary damage. It is proper in such instances to allow recovery for both items, provided there is no double recovery.

A second effect of the characterization of the injury is the application of the relevant statute of limitations. The statute of limitations period will begin running, unless tolled by equitable principles, from the date of the initial interference with the property. If the nature of the interference is a significant event that produces a permanent harm, the limitations period will be relatively predictable to calculate. A potential difficulty arises, though, where the interference with property is of a continuing character over a long period of time.

A common illustration involves a factory that is unlawfully discharging toxic effluent which leaches into the surrounding soil and contaminates an aquifer, affecting neighboring land uses. The question for landowners who seek damages for the resulting harm is whether the invasion rises to the level of a permanent harm, which then requires determining exactly when the statute of limitations began to run. Otherwise, it may be seen as a series of separate temporary harms stemming from the continuing pollution. If temporary, then the statute of limitations would run from each invasion.

Assume, for example, that the pollution continued for ten years before the landowner brought a suit for damages against the factory and further assume that the operative statute of limitations for torts is two years. If the harm is classified as permanent, then the landowner might be completely barred from any recovery if the trier of fact concludes that the first invasion constituted a permanent injury. On the other hand, if the injury is deemed temporary, then the landowner would be barred from recovering damages for the first eight years of harm but still could recover for any harms occurring within the previous two year period.

A third effect of the characterization is whether injunctive relief may be available. If the injury is classified as permanent, then courts will not issue a preventive injunction against the interference. The rationale is that the landowner is already being compensated for future harms through the diminution in value measure of damages. Therefore, an injunction to abate the harm in the future would be repetitive and overcompensate the plaintiff. In contrast, if the harm is temporary an injunction may potentially be issued. The damages given compensate for the past interference to the land and the injunction would prohibit future conduct, so there would be no inconsistency or overlap in the recovery.

A difference in cases involving real property from those involving personal property is that real property is never (or rarely) totally destroyed. Rather, some critical feature of the land may be injured, such as its productivity. If toxic chemicals leak into the soil or water on the land, then its productivity as farm land is injured. Consider an example where the blasting of dynamite for construction on neighboring land destroys the productivity of a well on the plaintiff's land. If it is not possible to drill for water on the land after the injury, then the damage was permanent. If that well can be restored, then repair costs are permissible, with states varying their rules about capping those damages. The most difficult question is how to categorize the injury if the current well cannot be repaired but another well could be dug on the same land. Courts have struggled with the problem of categorization between temporary and permanent injuries.

Injury to real property may also be to structures on the land. For the destruction of an improvement valuable separately from the land, the owner can recover its value at the time of destruction, less salvage value. If the structure is only damaged, cost of repair and loss of use is recoverable. Some courts will limit the cost of repairs to not exceed the diminution in the value of the improvements if it has a separate value, or to the diminution in the value of the entire land. Thus, if a car runs off the road and crashes into a shed on the plaintiff's land, the plaintiff receives cost of repair in most jurisdictions, with a cap on the value of the shed itself if it has separate value, such as a prefabricated shed bought at a retail store.

Damages are also recoverable for items, such as growing crops or fruit trees, that have a significant detached or severable value apart from the land. Injury to growing annual crops allows recovery of the projected commercial market value of the crop at maturity, less costs of harvesting and transportation that would otherwise have been incurred by the owner. Injury to land prepared for planting, however, enables a recovery of the cost of preparation, plus rental value for the season. Some types of property have their principal value in relation to the realty. For example, if the injured property is viewed as part of the land and has a special purpose to that land, such as ornamental trees, then the proper measure of damages would be diminution in value or possibly cost to restore if not excessive.

(C) Personal Injury Damages

A person who has been physically injured as a result of another's actionable conduct may recover damages that will fairly and reasonably compensate for the nature and extent of the injuries suffered. The goal of damages is to restore the injured party to the position, as nearly as practicable, prior to the tort. The damages must compensate for all detriment proximately caused by the wrongdoer's conduct. Damages may include recovery for both past and future losses. Damages for personal injury need not be calculated with mathematical certainty, but are designed to compensate for the losses sustained. Wide latitude of discretion is necessarily left to the jury, and the award will be upheld unless determined that the amount is so excessive as to indicate that bias, passion or prejudice influenced the jury.

Although jurisdictions vary somewhat in the allowable items of personal injury damages, the most common elements include: (1) lost earnings and impaired future earning capacity; (2) physical pain and suffering and mental distress; (3) medical expenses; (4) permanent injuries, disfigurement, or lasting destruction or impairment of health and physical functions; and (5) loss of consortium. Some items are classified as "general" damages, such as pain and suffering. Others are described as "special" damages, such as future medical expenses. The difference is that special damages must be pleaded and proved with particularity and typically require expert testimony to support the evidentiary record. General damages may be determined by the trier of fact based upon their own life experience and considering the nature of the injuries without the aid of expert testimony.

For permanent injuries, diminished future earning capacity is calculated for the time period of the injured party's work life expectancy. It takes into account both individualized factors, such as special skill and training, as well as broader industry factors and opportunities. The theory is to replace, as accurately as possible, the lost marketability in the workplace. Therefore, if a person's capacity to work has been diminished it will be compensable even if the injured party returns to the same job following the harm.

The injured party may also recover damages for medical expenses for past and future care and services. The medical costs expected for permanent injuries will be measured according to the injured party's projected life expectancy. The requirements for recovery of damages for medical care are that they are: (1) reasonable and necessary for proper treatment of the injuries sustained, (2) reasonable in amount, (3) that a causal relationship exists between the medical expenses and the injury itself, and (4) that any future costs are reasonably certain to be incurred. Future medical expenses, as an item of special damages, must be proven by expert testimony.

Pain and suffering of the victim is another item of general damages that may be awarded. The difficulty with allowing such recovery is providing some reasonable basis for determining an appropriate award since mental anguish is impossible to quantify. The jury typically will make such judgments based upon the nature and extent of any physical injuries. Principles of fair compensation still apply, so the jury award will be reviewed for excessiveness. Some jurisdictions recognize recovery for "loss of enjoyment of life" as a distinct element of damages. Psychological fears, such as post traumatic stress syndrome, may also be compensable but must be reasonable and may require expert testimony to supply an evidentiary foundation.

The claim for loss of consortium is a derivative claim brought by a spouse or some other family members. It is primarily based on the claimant's emotional suffering and thus considers: love, companionship, affection, society, comfort, services, and solace. The claim cannot be duplicative with other elements of the injured party's recovery, and does not include compensation for economic disadvantages or pecuniary losses. Some courts have expanded family members who may claim for loss of consortium beyond spouses. Some have recognized a cause of action by a minor child or incapacitated dependent child for permanent loss of parental consortium when a parent is negligently injured by a third party. Some have also permitted parents to claim loss of consortium with their minor children who are injured.

Future special damages should be discounted to present value, taking into account both the projected effects of investment of the damages award and inflation. Also, damages may be reduced by the failure of the injured party to properly mitigate by taking reasonable steps to secure prompt medical care and treatment. The allowance of prejudgment interest on some personal injury damages may be allowed, but often is governed by statute. Injured parties may recover the pecuniary losses even though they have been reimbursed for them from a collateral source such as medical or health insurance.

(D) Wrongful Death and Survival

At early common law, the prevailing view was that the death of a tort victim extinguished all of their potential claims against the tortfeasor. Further, the common law did not recognize any independent claim in the decedent's dependents for their own losses. In order to alleviate the harshness of this common law doctrine and to correct the anomalous result whereby tortfeasors could effectively "profit" from their wrong by actually killing the victim rather than just injuring them, England passed Lord Campbell's Act in 1846. This Act created a new and independent remedy for wrongful death in derogation of the common law preclusion. The Act has served as the model for numerous statutes promulgated in the United States. In many jurisdictions, a separate "survival" statute operates to preserve various personal injury claims that the victim would have been able to maintain, yet which would have been extinguished under the harsh common law approach. Some jurisdictions provide for recovery under wrongful death and survival statutes for the death of an unmarried, unemancipated minor child.

The wrongful death action has been merged in some jurisdictions with the survival statute under a single comprehensive statutory scheme. The purpose for merger of the two types of actions principally is one of administrative convenience and expediency in that the personal representative only has to maintain one lawsuit for wrongful death. There are some difficulties, however, in the single statutory approach, most notably in properly identifying and separating each item of damages to avoid double recovery.

The elements and measure of damages recoverable under the "survival" portion of the statutes mirror those traditionally available had the victim lived, other than future damages. Thus, mental pain and anguish of the decedent experienced prior to death would be typically recoverable under the survival statute.

Although jurisdictions differ in scope, many wrongful death statutes provide for the following elements: (1) pecuniary losses to the surviving spouse and children, (2) medical and burial expenses, and (3) loss of consortium and grief of the surviving spouse. Jurisdictions are divided as to whether punitive damages may be recovered. The element of pecuniary loss basically seeks to replace the financial support that the decedent would have otherwise given to their family. Accordingly, this item is calculated by taking into consideration the decedent's age, occupation, earning capacity, health habits, and probably duration of their life had the tort not occurred.

Any defenses that would have been otherwise available to the tortfeasor against the victim are also effectively preserved and may be properly asserted in the wrongful death action. Although the wrongful death statute creates a separate and distinct right of action to the decedent's legal representative against the wrongdoer, that right is predicated on the continued viability of rights which were personal to the deceased had he lived. Thus, wrongful death statutory claims are conditioned upon the existence of claims otherwise possessed by the decedent; consequently the ability to maintain a suit under the statute is derivative in character. Therefore, a wrongful death action would be precluded if the claims of the injured party were time-barred by an applicable statute of limitations prior to death.

Chapter 12

ADJUSTMENTS TO DAMAGES

(A) Present Value and Inflation

Compensatory damages that replace future losses, such as diminished earning capacity in a personal injury action, typically are awarded in a lump sum. The first step in calculating an award for lost earnings involves estimating the projected lost stream of income over the work life expectancy of the injured party. The lost income stream ordinarily is measured by after-tax dollars, and the discount rate represents the after-tax rate of return to the injured worker. *See* Norfolk & Western R. Co. v. Liepelt (S.Ct.1980).

The next step may involve adjusting the lump sum total by taking into account the impact of future inflation and discounting the award to present value. Both adjustments involve complex expert testimony of economic, industry, societal and individualized factors. The specific rates used for inflation and discounting may radically affect the final damages award given to the prevailing party. The selection of a higher inflation rate favors the plaintiff, while a higher discount rate would benefit the defendant.

Several different methods have emerged for evaluating the inflation and discount rates. The "total offset" method, premised upon the rationale that predicting future rates is inherently unreliable, simply cancels out both factors. The result is that the lump sum award is not adjusted once the damages are calculated.

A second approach is the "case by case" method, where experts introduce evidence on projected wage increases related to individualized and industry factors, including an enhancement for future inflation. The trier of fact then discounts that projected future lost income stream to present value using a market interest rate, which itself includes factors such as price inflation.

The third commonly used method is called the "varied offset" or "below-market" discount method. Evidence is considered on future hypothetical wage increases for the injured worker, taking into account both merit and industry productivity and market conditions. It leaves out the inflation factor, however, both with respect to future wages and interest rates. The resulting income stream is then discounted by a below-market discount rate between 1% and 3%, which is sometimes called the "real interest rate." This method was endorsed by the Supreme Court in *Jones & Laughlin Steel Corp. v. Pfeifer* (S.Ct.1983).

Another problem is the determination of the appropriate rate for discounting the lump sum. In *Pfeifer,* the Court stated that the discount rate should be based on the interest rate available on the "best and safest investments," which often are interpreted as federal government issued securities. The goal is to approximate the level of earnings that the money could earn through hypothetical investments that are relatively risk-free. In *Monessen Southwestern Ry. Co. v. Morgan* (S.Ct.1988), the Court stated that parties in a private suit may stipulate to the total offset method before trial, and thus avoid the inevitable battle of experts and uncertainties associated with predicting inflation and discount rates.

The calculation of future damages and adjustments to approximate interest rates and inflation necessarily present significant challenges to the parties, courts, and juries. The resulting award often may prove to be significantly higher or lower than the expert predictions in light of subsequent actual market events. In response to the potential inequity that could occur, an alternative method calls for the payment of damages in stages over the period of time that losses would be sustained. The Model Periodic Payment of Judgments Act provides a basic framework in which damages could be paid in installments as losses actually accrue. One benefit to the periodic payment of damages is that it alleviates the difficulties associated with making long term investment decisions of the lump sum award.

Regardless of whether the jurisdiction has approved periodic payment judgments, the parties may opt to have installment payments through private agreement, which is known as a "structured

settlement.'' Both parties often find it more satisfactory to negotiate for such periodic payments because the defendant can often purchase an annuity
for the plaintiff at less cost than the projected losses
and the plaintiff then has guaranteed payments for
a lifetime. Agreements can be as complex or simple
as the parties like, since a structured settlement is a
contract.

(B) Prejudgment Interest

Courts may award interest as an element of compensatory damages based upon statute, contract, or
through equitable discretion. State and federal statutes uniformly provide for the payment of post-
judgment interest to accrue on the damages awarded until paid. Parties may contract for payment of
conventional interest, such as in home and automobile loans and mortgages. More difficult questions
arise, however, with respect to the authorization of
prejudgment interest.

The prejudgment interest component of damages
compensates the prevailing party in a lawsuit for
the loss of use of the money that will later be
awarded at judgment. The award recognizes the
time value of money, because money itself has its
own earning power. The award focuses on the period from accrual of the claim until the date of
judgment. In that interim of time before damages
are actually awarded, the justification for paying
prejudgment interest is the recognition that the
claimant should be allowed some measure of interest on the sum of money later established at judg-

ment. Another policy reason for the award is that otherwise the liable party would be unjustly enriched by the interest earned on the funds and may delay settling or paying their obligations. Prejudgment interest is not a penalty in any sense; it is only compensation.

Two different issues exist with respect to prejudgment interest: entitlement and measurement. Various state and federal statutes include prejudgment interest as an allowable item of compensatory damages arising from violation of the statute. In those instances, the court often retains discretion as to whether interest should be given and to what extent. Similarly, parties have contractual freedom to incorporate a prejudgment interest component into their agreed menu of damages that would be payable to the non-breaching party in the event of a material breach of contract. The limitations on such provisions include ordinary considerations of unconscionability as well as statutory usury laws.

Apart from statute or agreement, though, courts retain considerable discretion to award prejudgment interest in order to achieve the objective of full and fair compensation. The court must evaluate a litany of factors, considering the matter from the perspective of both parties. The claimant must show the date of accrual of the claim, demonstrate that the claim may be calculated with a reasonable degree of certainty, and that the award is consistent with the goal of providing full compensation. The court will also consider whether the defendant would be unjustly enriched by not paying interest, and evaluate whether the defendant may have acted to delay the trial or the payment of the claim. Good faith efforts by the defendant to resolve the dispute by offering settlement may operate to toll the running of interest as to the amount of settlement offered.

Instances where liability itself or the amount of the claim are very uncertain often may be less likely to justify a prejudgment interest award. Otherwise, the defendant may be placed in a dilemma of either being forced to pay a legitimately disputed claim or having to pay interest on the claim after judgment is rendered. As a result, courts historically espoused the notion that "liquidated" claims were proper subjects for prejudgment interest, while those which were not readily ascertainable were not. The modern view generally discards the requirement that the claim be liquidated, yet the underlying premise of showing the merits and the amount of entitlement with reasonable certainty still affects the court's discretion.

A degree of flexibility is generally employed by courts to tailor the prejudgment interest award to the nature of the claim itself. For example, in breach of contracts cases the date of the breach and measure of damages often is fairly readily calculable with relative certainty. Accordingly, prejudgment interest could be awarded with respect to the compensatory damages attributable to the breach and would not be unduly prejudicial to the breaching party. In other instances, interest may be awarded to serve the goal of just compensation. *See* Restatement (Second) of Contracts § 354.

On the other hand, with respect to various torts claims, the question of liability and amount of harm, may be less certain. Therefore, interest generally may not be awarded for emotional distress, bodily injury, pain and suffering, and injury to reputation claims. *See* Restatement (Second) of Torts § 913. If the injury has a readily ascertainable market value, such as for destruction of personalty, prejudgment interest may be awarded. Interest also is typically not awarded on punitive damages because it does not accord with the objective of compensation to the claimant. Courts also do not award interest on future losses because they have not yet been incurred.

The second issue courts must resolve is determining the appropriate rate to use for the prejudgment interest award. Unless the applicable statute or contract delineates the rate of interest, courts will exercise their discretion guided by reference to a market-based rate. The goal is to approximate the lost opportunity that the claimant would have had to invest the funds. A common reference point is a high grade government fixed income bond, such as United States Treasury Bills or money market rates offered by major institutions.

Chapter 13

LIMITATIONS ON COMPENSATORY DAMAGES

(A) Foreseeability

Foreseeability is a limitation on all compensatory damages, both in contract and in tort. It functions to prevent liability for unlimited loss, because otherwise the consequences from a tort or breach of contract could be limitless. The concept of foreseeability operates in different ways under different substantive law, but the overall purpose is the same.

The requirement of foreseeability in contract reflects a policy of fairness in that a party will be held accountable only for those risks that should have been reasonably foreseeable at the time of making the agreement. The principles underlying the doctrine in commercial contracts were highlighted in a famous early English case of *Hadley v. Baxendale* (1854). In that case an engine shaft in the plaintiff's mill broke, so he hired a common carrier to transport the part to the manufacturer in order to obtain a replacement part based on the original design. The carrier delayed in delivering the part to the manufacturer, causing the mill to shut down for a period of time. The plaintiff sued the carrier for lost profits associated with the stoppage of the mill. The court denied the claim on the basis that the defendant carrier did not have notice of the special circumstances involved in the contract for carriage. The court reasoned that the damages must relate to what fairly and reasonably would arise naturally, either based upon the contract itself or what would reasonably be contemplated by the parties at the time of contract formation. Because the nature or terms of the contract did not provide sufficient notice of the potential liability for delayed performance, foreseeability was not satisfied.

The *Hadley* doctrine has been carried forward in the common law as well as under the Uniform Commercial Code. It limits liability for losses that were not reasonably foreseeable by the breaching party at the time of contracting. *See* Restatement (Second) of Contracts § 351 comment a; comment 2; U.C.C. § 2–715(2)(a). The doctrine requires an inquiry into what knowledge or understanding the breaching party reasonably should be charged with at the time of contract formation. *Hadley* reflects the policy choice in contract that breaching parties are held responsible only for those risks that they fairly have assumed and that were contemplated as part of bargained-for exchanges. As it is most commonly interpreted, the rule is predicated on an objective examination of the nature of the contract. It requires inferences of what the breaching party should have known, not what subjectively or actually might have been understood. Accordingly, evidence of the relationship of the parties, the nature and purpose of the contract, custom and trade usage, course of dealing, and sophistication of the parties may be relevant in determining foreseeability.

The principle of foreseeability applies to all types of contract damages, although with varying restrictiveness depending on the nature of the contract and the damages sought. The common law rule provides that general damages will be awarded for harms that flow directly and immediately as a natural consequence of the kind of non-performance by the breaching party. The law conclusively presumes such damages to be reasonably contemplated by the breaching party simply by virtue of the type of breach. For example, the delivery of something of lesser quality or quantity at variance from the contract terms obviously diminishes the value of the bargain and deserves appropriate compensation. Under the U.C.C. such damages are illustrated by the provision allowing an aggrieved buyer to recover damages for the difference in value for accepted but non-conforming goods. See § 2–714.

Foreseeability presents a significant limitation in circumstances where the non-breaching party seeks special or consequential damages, such as lost profits. For example, the claimant may assert that the non-performance under one contract caused a loss of profits under a second contract with a third party. In that situation, the claimant must show that the breaching party should have contemplated or foreseen that the failure in performance in one contract caused the lost profits in the second. Under

U.C.C. § 2–715(2), recovery of consequential damages is based upon whether at the time of contracting the seller had "reason to know" of general or particular requirements of the buyer. The Code rejects the restrictive "tacit-agreement" test under older common law where the breaching party would be accountable only for non-performance terms that were specifically assumed. *See* § 2–715 comment 2.

The doctrine of foreseeability also plays a significant role in tort law, although in a different fashion than in contract law. In torts, foreseeability initially functions in defining the nature and extent of the duty owed in ascertaining negligence. The assessment of foreseeability requires a hindsight analysis of what the alleged tortfeasor should have reasonably anticipated would have been the categorical harm that would result from their actions at the time of the injury. Accordingly, it is a hypothetical construct because it asks the objective question of what a reasonable person should have realized, not what the particular defendant actually contemplated.

In the United States, the use of foreseeability to define tort duty was articulated by Justice Cardozo in the leading case, *Palsgraf v. Long Island Railroad Company* (N.Y.1928). In *Palsgraf,* a railroad employee tried to help a passenger board a moving train by pushing him from behind. The passenger dropped a small package containing fireworks, which exploded when they fell. The explosion caused a nearby scale to fall and strike the plaintiff, who was standing nearby on a railroad platform. She sued the railroad for negligence.

The majority opinion held that the railroad employee's actions had negligently endangered the passenger who was trying to board the train but did not foreseeably place the injured plaintiff at risk. Therefore there was no breach of a duty owed to her. Cardozo explained that "the orbit of the danger as disclosed to the eye of reasonable vigilance would be the orbit of the duty." Further, he observed "the risk reasonably to be perceived defines the duty to be obeyed and risk imports relation; it is risk to another or to others within the range of apprehension." Because the sequence of events leading to the injury were so highly extraordinary, the railroad did not breach its duty of care to the plaintiff.

The dissenting opinion by Justice Andrews in *Palsgraf* objected to the majority's use of foreseeability to limit recovery so severely. The case is famous for presenting the opposing views on the proper role of foreseeability in tort. The Andrews approach, followed in many jurisdictions, is to trace the foreseeability of consequences that flow from the accident itself. Under this view, the plaintiff would be able to show that she was in close enough proximity to the explosion of fireworks to make her injury one that flowed naturally from the events as they unfolded.

The significance of the difference between the Cardozo and Andrews views in *Palsgraf* is twofold. First, the Cardozo view disfavors liability more than the Andrews view. Second, the Cardozo approach makes the issue of foreseeability a question of law for the court rather than a question of fact for the jury. The rejection of the duty approach by Andrews has the effect of making the question of foreseeability a factual inquiry.

It is universally said that a tortfeasor does not have to anticipate the exact manner, means or extent of the harm. As long as the conduct is a substantial factor in producing an injury that is not too remote, the actor will be accountable for the foreseeable consequences. *See* Restatement (Second) Torts § 435. Under the "thin-skulled" or "egg-shell" plaintiff rule, a tortfeasor will be responsible for severe consequences to a particularly frail or susceptible person even if a normal person may not have experienced the same degree of harm. *See* Dulieu v. White (K.B.1901). The rationale is that tort liability focuses on the reasonably foreseeable type or category of harm, not the exact extent of injury produced.

Foreseeability requirements also limit damages for remote injuries under the doctrine of proximate cause, which is also called legal cause. This restriction reflects a policy judgment that liability should not be extended for unforeseeably remote injuries, even if they were caused in fact by the tortfeasor. Tort law balances the need for compensation with a concern that excessive damages would be inefficient and not socially desirable.

The tension between the goals of compensation and efficiency has resulted in a variety of treatments of proximate cause. An early leading English opinion, *In re Polemis* (K.B.1921), took the extreme position in favor of compensation and held that tort liability would extend to all injuries directly caused by the negligent conduct. This rule rejected the foreseeability requirement because it imposed liability even if the actor could not have reasonably anticipated the harmful consequences. That position was later rejected by another Commonwealth decision, known as *The Wagon Mound, No. 1* [1961]. In that case, Viscount Simonds observed that "it does not seem consonant with current ideas of justice or morality that for an act of negligence, however slight or venial, which results in some trivial foreseeable damage the actor should be liable for all consequences however unforeseeable and however grave, so long as they can be said to be 'direct.' " Instead, the court determined that negligence should depend on the foreseeability of the consequent harm even if it was only remotely foreseeable. In American jurisdictions courts have tended to favor rules that require "reasonable foreseeability" of the consequences of torts for the satisfaction of proximate cause.

The predominant view in modern law is that foreseeability is a significant limiting doctrine in both tort and contract. As such, foreseeability embodies notions of fairness to strike a proper balance between the goals of compensation and of limitation to keep damages within appropriate boundaries. In the absence of foreseeability requirements, tortfeasors and breaching parties to contracts would be accountable for losses that they could not have reasonably contemplated. Modern law does not extend the principle of providing just compensation so far as to make breaching parties and tortfeasors absolute insurers for all losses, however remote or unexpected.

(B) Certainty

Another limitation on both entitlement and measurement of compensatory damages is the requirement that they must be proven with reasonable certainty. The standard is stated in terms of reasonableness rather than mathematical precision, and therefore is satisfied where a rational basis exists for computation.

Several principles guide the trier-of-fact in determining whether the proof offered satisfies the plaintiff's burden. First, as a matter of fundamental fairness, the injured party bears the burden of demonstrating that all claimed damages are caused by and traceable to the tortious conduct at issue or the breach of contract asserted. Second, the compensatory damages must satisfy the objective of fair compensation rather than punishment for the behavior. Finally, recognition is given to the reality that certain types of injuries are inherently less capable of empirical proof than others. There is considerable latitude given with respect to the certainty requirement for certain losses, such as pain and suffering or emotional distress. In contrast, a fairly high quantum of reliable evidence is needed for proof of lost profits associated with breach of contract. *See* Restatement (Second) of Torts § 912. In situations where the plaintiff has established a violation of a right but somehow has not shown the damages with appropriate degree of certainty, the trier of fact may award nominal damages to vindicate the infringement of the legal interest.

In the context of torts, another reason for liberalizing the standard for certainty is the policy that the wrongdoer should not profit from the very uncertainty that their conduct created. Stated alternatively, tort law seeks to provide compensation and redress for harms but also reflects a social judgment that the tortfeasor should be held accountable for their behavior and that damages awarded may deter others in the future from similar conduct. Accordingly, once the plaintiff demonstrates entitlement to some damages, courts will generally provide a measure of leeway on the certainty limitation with regard to the amount of damages. *See* Story Parchment Co. v. Paterson Parchment Paper Co. (S.Ct. 1931).

The certainty requirement presents particular challenges to plaintiffs also where they seek lost profits for breach of contract involving a new business venture. The traditional approach disallows recovery of such profits where no prior operating history exists. Some courts, though, have considered comparable enterprises or the limited operational history and awarded lost profits. *See* Lehrman v. Gulf Oil Corp. (5th Cir.1974).

The Uniform Commercial Code maintains a policy of liberally applying remedies, and therefore rejects the view that "damages must be calculable with mathematical accuracy." *See* Comment 1 to U.C.C. § 1–106. Instead, the U.C.C. embraces a flexible approach where compensatory damages need only be proven in whatever manner is reasonable under the circumstances. *See* Comment 4 to U.C.C. § 2–715. Also, the Code incorporates the common law doctrinal guidance of proving damages by a reasonableness standard. See U.C.C. § 1–103.

(C) Avoidable Consequences

The doctrine of mitigation or avoidable consequences is another limitation on compensatory damages. The rule operates to limit recovery when an injured party has failed to take reasonable steps to avoid or limit further losses following upon incurrence of harm. The doctrine applies in all areas of law as a basic principle of compensatory damages.

The obligation of the innocent party is often couched in terms of a "duty", but that characterization is somewhat misleading because the failure to meet the standard of reasonable mitigation does not result in a breach leading to damages. Instead, the failure to mitigate serves to exclude any damages that may be sustained following the failure to undertake reasonable steps following the harm. Restatement (Second) of Torts § 918 comment a. In that sense, the doctrine operates negatively by denying recovery of certain damages that a non-breaching party could have otherwise reasonably avoided without excessive risk or burden. See Restatement (Second) of Contracts § 350. The rule also functions affirmatively by allowing recovery of costs incurred in effecting mitigation.

The doctrine of avoidable consequences reflects three primary policy goals. First, it embodies notions of fairness to breaching parties or tortfeasors by holding them accountable only for damages resulting from their actions. Second, it protects the innocent party by affirmatively enabling them to undertake reasonable avoidance measures, such as seeking substitute employment or obtaining replacement goods following a contract breach, in order to secure their justifiable expectations. Finally, the rule advances a public policy of avoiding economic waste through excessive damages.

A frequent problem is applying the standard of reasonableness for purposes of mitigation. Non-breaching parties do not have to undertake extraordinary measures or suffer inconvenience or hardship in attempting to mitigate losses. Nor must they necessarily be successful in the mitigation attempt. The doctrine of mitigation promotes diligence, but does not necessarily require that a non-breaching party successfully obtain a replacement job or find substitute goods. Further, a injured party is entitled to reimbursement of expenses reasonably incurred in attempting to mitigate losses even if those efforts are unsuccessful.

In tort law, the doctrine of mitigation obligates an injured party to exercise the care of a person of ordinary intelligence and prudence under similar circumstances. That may include undergoing surgical or medical treatment within a reasonable time to minimize damages. Whether or not a specific medical procedure is deemed reasonable will involve an assessment of many factors, including the nature and extent of the risks presented, the likelihood of success, alternatives to surgery, the state of medical knowledge, the degree of possible complications arising from the procedure, and the expenditure of money or effort required. *See* Lobermeier v. General Telephone Company of Wisconsin (Wis.1984). Although an injured party is never required to undergo recommended medical treatment, such as elective surgery, a tortfeasor may not be held accountable for damages resulting from a disability or pain if medical treatment could have reasonably cured the condition. The tortfeasor bears the burden of pleading and proving failure to mitigate as an affirmative defense.

In contracts, once a party breaches a construction contract by giving unequivocal notice of repudiation, the non-breaching party cannot recover damages for work performed following the receipt of the cancellation notice. The non-breaching party has a duty of mitigation that contemplates ceasing performance so as not to unduly increase the damages. *See* Rockingham County v. Luten Bridge Co. (4th Cir.1929).

The concept of what constitutes a reasonable substitute may present particular problems in the context of employment contracts. For example, in *Parker v. Twentieth Century–Fox Film Corporation*

(Cal.1970), an actress successfully claimed that it was not a reasonable substitute to accept a leading role in a western motion picture to be produced in Australia when the studio breached an employment contract for her services to perform in a musical production in California. The court reasoned that the artist was not required to seek or accept employment that was "different or inferior" in order to mitigate damages.

The Uniform Commercial Code also incorporates the doctrine of avoidable consequences, and will limit the amount of damages potentially recoverable if the non-breaching party fails to take reasonable measures to mitigate following a material breach. *See* U.C.C. §§ 2–708; 2–713; 2–610 comment 1. In *Oloffson v. Coomer* (Ill. App.1973), for example, a grain dealer unreasonably delayed in seeking to obtain replacement goods following notice of the seller's breach. As a result, the aggrieved buyer could not recover damages that could have been avoided by purchasing substitute goods in a timely manner.

(D) Collateral Source Rule

Two principles of tort law that sometimes collide are (1) that responsible parties should be accountable for the losses caused by their wrongful conduct, and (2) that damages should place injured parties effectively in the same position as they stood prior to the tortious conduct. When an injured party receives payment from a source other than the defendant, the second principle will be violated if there is double coverage for the same harm. If that amount from a third party is deducted from damages, however, the first principle is violated.

All payments made by the responsible party to the plaintiff, whether made prior to or following formal adjudication of liability, are credited to offset the damages owed. In some instances, the injured party may also receive payments or benefits from other sources, such as from insurance, as a direct consequence of the injury. The question then becomes whether or not such collateral or third-party payments should offset the ultimate tort liability of the wrongdoer.

The traditional formulation of the collateral source rule provides that if an injured party receives compensation or benefits from a source unaffiliated or independent from the tortfeasor, then those payments will not be deducted from the damages the plaintiff otherwise may be entitled to collect from the wrongdoer. *See* Restatement (Second) of Torts, § 920A (1979); Helfend v. Southern California Rapid Transit Dist. (Cal.1970). The rule further operates to exclude the introduction of evidence of ancillary benefits or compensation received by the claimant as a result of the injury to avoid prejudice with the jury. *See* Fitzgerald v. Expressway Sewerage Const., Inc. (1st Cir.1999).

The rule has been applied in a variety of contexts, including the receipt of insurance proceeds, employment benefits, gifts of money or medical services, welfare benefits, and tax advantages.

The collateral source rule generally does not apply with the same force in contract cases, because the nature of the benefit of the bargain is met either by performance or payment of damages, and third party insurance for nonperformance ordinarily does not come into play.

The collateral source rule has drawn considerable criticism in recent years, principally on the grounds that it can lead to a double recovery or a windfall to the injured party. If so, the rule undermines the principle of just compensation associated with the goal of placing the injured party in the same position held prior to the harm.

Supporters of the rule assert that it retains vitality for several reasons. First, an injured party should be entitled to receive the benefits of their insurance policy because they have contracted for coverage and should properly be compensated for losses associated with the risks contemplated. Otherwise, it could create a disincentive to obtain insurance coverage because an injured party would have paid premiums yet not received compensation for the very risks covered by the policy. The double recovery argument also is countered by the reality that most insurance policies include a subrogation provision whereby the plaintiff is paid for their losses and then the insurance company "stands in their shoes" seeking reimbursement from the tortfeasor.

Another policy argument favoring retention of the rule is that if any windfall does result, it should enjoyed by the innocent party rather than the one responsible for the harm. Similarly, the rule is supported on the grounds that a tortfeasor should be liable for full compensatory damages, without an offset, in order to carry out the social goals of deterrence and accountability. Some have also suggested an indirect justification in that the rule provides an economic offset to the attorneys' fees owed by the plaintiff. *See* McLean v. Runyon (9th Cir.2000).

One of the complexities in applying the collateral source rule has been determining whether or not a source should be viewed as affiliated with or independent from the tortfeasor. For example, classification of some governmental or public sector benefits, such as medicare or unemployment compensation, have presented particular difficulties of application.

Another problem area has been the issue of whether an injured party should be permitted to recover the reasonable value of gratuitously rendered services or benefits. Some courts have held that the rule still applies and the injured party is entitled to recover the reasonable market value of medical costs, even if actually provided by a collateral source at a below market rate or gratuitously. *See* Restatement (Second) of Torts § 920A, comment c (1979). A justification for this approach is to carry out the intent of the donor to benefit the injured party rather than the tortfeasor. *See* Hueper v. Goodrich (Minn.1982). The contrary view favoring an offset reasons that the purposes of fair compensation outweigh the application of the rule and have reduced a damages award accordingly.

In recent years, the collateral source rule has proved to be a fertile subject for state tort reform. Although states vary widely in their formulation of policy, some modifications include: allowing evidence pertaining to payments from collateral courses, requiring the jury to consider collateral benefits in assessing damages, and reducing a damages award.

Chapter 14

DAMAGES FOR ECONOMIC LOSS OR DISTRESS ALONE

(A) Economic Loss Damages

One traditional rule of tort damages is that no recovery is allowed for negligently inflicted economic losses absent physical harm to person or property. Also, purely economic losses are generally not recoverable under strict products liability. *See* Seely v. White Motor Co. (Cal.1965); Restatement (Second) of Torts, § 402A (1965). The issue may arise where a negligent act causes an interference with the performance of another's contractual duties and the resulting harm is of a solely economic nature, such as lost profits. Contract law may provide incomplete relief to compensate for the losses sustained due to restrictions like warranty, privity, and disclaimers or limitations of liability. Accordingly, if contract law does not allow an avenue for compensation for the damages sustained, the question becomes whether tort law offers a remedial alternative.

Defective products that may cause personal injury or property damage may justify compensation for damages through either negligence or strict liability theories of § 402A of the Restatement (Second) of Torts. Further, buyers of defective products may recover under express or implied warranty for losses associated with the diminished value or failure to meet performance. Also, if personal injury or property damage are incurred as a result of the negligence, then pecuniary losses which are "parasitic" to the injuries may also be recoverable. See Restatement (Second) of Torts § 766C comment b. Therefore, any economic losses are only recoverable in negligence when the claimant suffers specific tangible harms to person or property.

Courts have stated various justifications for the *per se* rule precluding recovery of economic losses for negligent interference with contractual relations absent physical harm to person or property. Some base the result on duty analysis, or find the loss too remote or indirect to satisfy proximate cause. Others reason that a bright-line rule is necessary to avoid imposition of disproportionate damages relative to the fault involved.

An early expression of the absolute bar approach was followed in the leading case of *Robins Dry Dock & Repair Co. v. Flint* (S.Ct.1927). A steamship charterer sought to recover lost profits attributable to delays when the defendant negligently broke a vessel's propeller. The charterer had a contract with the ship's owners but did not have a property interest in the ship itself. The Court denied recovery of economic losses potentially attributable to the delay, reasoning "The law does not spread its protection so far." The Restatement (Second) of Torts adopted the approach of the Court in *Robins Dry Dock*. It denies recovery for pecuniary losses resulting from a negligent interference with contractual performance (§ 766C), but allows compensation if the tortfeasor intentionally interfered with performance (§ 766A) or with prospective contractual relations (§ 766B).

Although an absolute bar rule provides predictability and certainty, it also has been criticized for producing harsh or unfortunate results in some cases. One of the chief criticisms is that even provable economic losses that are directly traceable to the negligent conduct would be denied or potentially recoverable depending upon the fortuity of whether a property loss occurred as well. The extent of the personal injury or property loss is not controlling but rather that one occurred. Consequently, some courts have recognized narrow exceptions for recovery where the parties had a "special relationship." For example, in *Union Oil Co. v. Oppen* (9th Cir. 1974), the court held that commercial fishermen could recover lost profits resulting from an oil spill caused by the defendants, finding a special duty owed to the foreseeable class of plaintiffs.

(B) Distress Damages

Remedial issues with distress damages arise when the plaintiff has established an action for the invasion of another interest. In a claim for invasion of an interest in person or property, distress damages are recoverable as "parasitic damages." The limits on such recovery are governed by the limitations of foreseeability and certainty. Foreseeable distress and its consequences are usually traced quite liberally in personal injury cases, as a matter of the pain and suffering award. In cases involving torts such as fraud or conversion, jurisdictions generally interpret foreseeability restrictively or prohibit such damages altogether.

Claims involving damages only for emotional distress are disfavored as a matter of substantive law, in addition to the remedial restrictions on such damages. The general rule in negligence law is that there is no substantive claim for negligently caused distress without physical injury. There are also exceptions to the tort rule, notably including the "witness" cases where plaintiffs suffer distress from viewing an injury to a loved one. In most states, witness plaintiffs who were in the zone of danger of the accident may recover for their distress in watching harm to a loved one. Some states allow recovery to distressed witnesses even if the claimant is not in the zone of danger but apply other foreseeability restrictions.

In contract law, the general rule is that a contract claim will not support distress damages unless those damages were reasonably within the contemplation of the contracting parties when the agreement was made. There are a few exceptions. The *Restatement (Second) of Contracts* § 353 provides for distress damages in contract only if "the breach also caused bodily harm or the contract or the breach is of such a kind that serious emotional disturbance was a particularly likely result." Examples of the latter category include (1) contracts between carriers and passengers, (2) contracts between innkeepers and guests, (3) contracts to handle dead bodies, such as for transportation or disposal, and (4) contracts for the delivery of messages concerning death. Unless a case fails to fall within one of the narrow exceptions to distress damages for breach of contract, there is no recovery unless the plaintiff can also establish an independent tort.

Chapter 15

PUNITIVE DAMAGES

(A) Entitlement

Punitive damages is the area of civil damages that overlaps with criminal law in its purpose and function. Unlike compensatory damages, punitive damages are not awarded to plaintiffs to compensate for their losses. Rather, punitive damages are awarded to punish defendants for egregious conduct and deter defendants and others from future offenses. Punitive damages are often referred to as "exemplary damages" because they are intended to make defendants public examples of inappropriate behavior. Punitive damages also are sometimes referred to as "smart money" because they are supposed to hurt defendants financially.

Punitive damages have a lengthy heritage in Anglo–American jurisprudence. American courts began to recognize punitive damage awards at least as early as 1791. Proponents argue that punitive damages are necessary to assess the true societal costs of defendants' misfeasances. An award of punitive damages also provides a fund from which plaintiffs can recover attorneys fees and other litigation costs that are otherwise noncompensable. Despite their longstanding presence, however, punitive damages remain a controversial issue.

One of the chief criticisms of punitive damages is that they are quasi-criminal in character in punishing defendants for anti-social conduct, yet are imposed without the benefit of traditional constitutional safeguards that apply in criminal trials. Further, the awards provide a windfall to successful plaintiffs and therefore transcend the objective of compensating for injuries. Additional concerns are that juries are given too much discretion in deciding on the entitlement and measurement of punitive awards. The incentive of receiving large punitive damage awards also may encourage unnecessary litigation, further diminishing valuable judicial resources. Punitive damages pose special problems in mass disaster and products liability cases. Courts are challenged in those cases to accommodate the goals of punishment and deterrence without imposing ruinous liability. Finally, some contend that the awards simple are ineffective in achieving the stated goals of punishment and deterrence, especially where a wrongdoer may shift the loss through insurance.

A claim for punitive damages is not considered an independent cause of action but is derivative in character. Therefore, although the elements of proof differ for punitive and compensatory damages, entitlement to an exemplary award is dependent upon the success of the underlying claim. As a general rule, punitive damages are not awarded in equity. With the merger of law and equity, however, some courts have recognized such damages in appropriate cases.

Punitive damages are not available to redress all legal wrongs. Instead, the purpose of such awards is to punish and deter only egregiously bad conduct. Jurisdictions vary in defining the standard of conduct that may support entitlement to punitive damages. The traditional approach authorizes punitive damages where (a) the defendant's conduct reflects a subjective malicious intent or acts with an evil motive, or (b) or objectively demonstrates gross recklessness or a willful disregard for the rights of others. The intent necessary to maintain an action for an intentional tort is not identical with the frame of mind of the wrongdoer necessary to recover punitive damages. Intentional torts are premised upon deliberate conduct that is substantially certain to invade the plaintiff's legally protected interest. The defendant may even have good intentions and yet be liable for an intentional tort. For punitive damages, however, the majority of jurisdictions require an "evil mind" or "malice."

(B) Punitive Damages for Breach of Contract

The prevailing rule is that punitive damages are ordinarily not recoverable for breach of a contractual obligation unless the conduct also constitutes an independent tort which would support such an award. See Restatement (Second) of Contracts § 355 (1981). Various justifications explain the traditional rule of denying punitive damages for breach of contract.

One rationale is that punitive damages are imposed to vindicate public rather than private rights. Thus, society's interest in punishing and deterring the behavior that support exemplary damages are not advanced for mere contract breach. Further, the nature of the bargain itself in contract law reflects an expectation for performance or compensation for damages resulting from breach. The underlying purpose of damages for breach of contract is to place the non-breaching party in the same position as if full performance had been rendered. Contract law does not inquire into subjective intent or attach moral blame for non-performance of promises. Further, punitive damages could undermine the theory of efficient breach, allowing the breaching party to pay damages while maximizing their own profits.

The presence of an independent tort to justify punitive damages for breach of contract is not actually an "exception" to the general rule, but rather a recognition that the same course of conduct can potentially give rise to alternative or cumulative causes of action sounding in contract or tort. In recent years, some courts have displayed an increased willingness to find sufficiently tortious conduct accompanying the contract breach to support an award of punitive damages.

A majority of jurisdictions hold that a breach of the implied covenant of good faith and fair dealing, either under common law or the Uniform Commercial Code, is not a tort sufficiently independent enough of the obligations required by the contract to allow for the imposition of punitive damages.

A growing trend recognizes an exception to the general rule to allow punitive damages predicated upon the bad faith conduct of insurance companies with respect to policy coverage or claims. These cases draw upon the public interest considerations that were expressed in an early line of cases that allowed punitive damages against common carriers and fiduciaries in limited situations. Courts have considered the special relationship between insurer and insured, the unequal bargaining power of the parties, and the adhesive nature of the insurance contract as public policy reasons to support punitive damages. A handful of courts also have found similar justifications to allow employees to recover punitive damages for an employer's breach of the covenant of good faith and fair dealing implied in an employment contract.

(C) Measurement

Punitive damages are never awarded automatically, nor as a matter of right. The trier of fact has discretion both with respect to determining entitlement and measurement of such damages. Although jurisdictions vary in the formulation of relevant factors guiding measurement of punitive damages, certain factors are commonly used. Those factors include: (a) the defendant's financial condition, including whether defendant profited financially from its actions; (b) the nature and reprehensibility of defendant's conduct; (c) the seriousness of the harm resulting from the misconduct; (d) the defendant's awareness and motivation regarding the potential harm; (e) the duration of the harm and any efforts to conceal the misconduct; (f) the total deterrent effect of other damages and punishment imposed upon the defendant, and (g) the extent that the conduct offends the public sense of justice.

The financial condition of the defendant is an appropriate consideration because the purpose of an award of punitive damages is to punish and deter the defendant and others similarly situated from engaging in such conduct in the future. The other factors are more directly related to the conduct that gave rise to the claim and the public interest. A reviewing court will not set aside an award of punitive damages unless it is so excessive that it appears to be the result of "passion or prejudice" or "shocks the judicial conscience".

Many jurisdictions require that punitive damages bear some reasonable relationship to the underlying compensatory damages award. However, no fixed ratio or proportion is mandated under common law principles. This limitation creates special problems in many civil rights cases where the plaintiff has not suffered pecuniary or physical harm from the violation.

The Supreme Court held in *Carey v. Piphus* (S.Ct. 1978) that nominal damages are an appropriate way to vindicate the deprivation of procedural due process rights where actual damages are not shown. A substantial number of jurisdictions have held that nominal damages can support an award of punitive damages. The rationale is that the aims of punitive damages are to punish and deter certain types of misconduct rather than to compensate. Restatement (Second) of Torts § 908 comment c. Further, certain intentional acts do not require showing of actual damages, yet nevertheless may support punitive damages due to the special circumstances surrounding the misconduct. A few jurisdictions, however, require that a jury must award a plaintiff compensatory damages in order to support a punitive damages award.

Special problems arise when there are multiple potential plaintiffs harmed by one defendant, such as in products liability cases. The wealth or poverty of the defendant is an important factor in setting the level of punitive damages because the purpose of the award is to punish and to deter the defendant and others similarly situated from such conduct in the future. In products liability cases, the financial condition of the company may be evaluated by focusing on the profits earned from marketing an unsafe product in reckless disregard of public safety. This rationale deteriorates when multiple cases seek to deprive the defendant of the same profit. At some point, the collective awards of punitive damages transcend the objective of punishment and deterrence and may threaten the viability of the enterprise. Additional concerns involve creating a "race to the courthouse" for recovery of punitive damages. Another criticism is that multiple punitive awards may substantially deplete corporate funds such that some injured parties may go compensated for legitimate claims. As a consequence, some jurisdictions take into account previous punitive awards imposed for the same conduct.

Some legislative reform measures have sought to limit admissibility of information regarding a defendant's financial condition. These measures generally bifurcate the trial and require a finding of entitlement to punitive damages before a jury may consider evidence of a defendant's financial worth. The policy reason for requiring a plaintiff to demonstrate entitlement to punitive damages before offering evidence of financial condition is to avoid prejudicing the jury with "punitive" evidence, thus inflating a compensatory award.

(D) Vicarious Liability

Jurisdictions are split as to whether a principal can be held vicariously liable for punitive damages based on an agent's tortious conduct. Some permit the principal to be liable for punitive damages solely on the basis of the conduct of the agent. The majority view follows the strict "complicity liability" theory where the principal generally is not liable for punitive damages absent authorization, participation, or ratification of the agent's tortious conduct.

The Restatement (Second) of Torts § 909 advances a broader scope of vicarious liability for punitive damages by including situations involving the reckless employment of an unfit agent and acts within the scope of employment by agents serving in a managerial capacity. *Accord* Restatement (Second) of Agency § 217C. The rationale for the Re-

statement position is twofold: to encourage diligence in the selection and supervision of persons
placed in management positions and to serve as a
deterrent to the employment of unfit persons for
important positions. Restatement (Second) of Torts
§ 909 comment b. Some jurisdictions follow the
more liberal "vicarious liability" rule that allow
imposition of punitive damages against a principal
for the wrongful conduct of agents acting within the
scope of the actor's authority.

(E) Constitutional Limits

The Supreme Court has devoted considerable attention in the past few years to various constitutional questions pertaining to punitive damages. In
Browning-Ferris Industries v. Kelco Disposal, Inc.
(S.Ct.1989) the Court held the Excessive Fines
Clause of the Eighth Amendment did not apply to a
civil jury award of punitive damages in civil cases
between private parties. The Court concluded that
although the goals of punishment and deterrence
underlie both punitive awards and criminal law, the
extent of any overlap was not sufficient to impose
the same constitutional limitations.

The Court held in *Pacific Mut. Life Ins. Co. v.
Haslip* (S.Ct.1991) that the Constitution imposes a
substantive limit on the size of punitive damage
awards. In that case the Court addressed a due
process challenge to Alabama's common law method
and procedures for assessing and reviewing punitive
damages. The jury had awarded $840,000 in puni-
tive damages in the case, which involved a claim

against an insurance company for the fraudulent actions of its agent. That amount was approximately four times the compensatory damages awarded and over 200 times the claimant's actual out-of-pocket expenses. Justice Blackmun, writing for the majority, raised concerns that punitive damages have "run wild" with unlimited jury and judicial discretion, yet declined to establish a "mathematical bright line" for constitutionally acceptable awards. The Court upheld the state's standards in the case, finding that due process requirements were satisfied where the discretion was exercised within "reasonable constraints."

Subsequently the Supreme Court held that the Due Process Clause of the Fourteenth Amendment prohibits a State from imposing a "grossly excessive" punishment on a tortfeasor. In *TXO Production Corp. v. Alliance Resources Corp.* (S.Ct.1993) the Court considered the due process implications of a $10 million punitive damage award in a common law slander of title action where only $19,000 in actual damages were awarded. The Court again declined to adopt any bright line test, but held that where "fair procedures were followed" an exemplary award was entitled to a strong presumption of validity. In addition to proportionality of punitives to actual damages, the Court also recognized the magnitude of potential harm and incentive for gain to the defendant as relevant factors. The plurality of the Court approved of the following illustration:

> For instance, a man wildly fires a gun into a crowd. By sheer chance, no one is injured and the

only damage is to a $10 pair of glasses. A jury reasonably could find only $10 in compensatory damages, but thousands of dollars in punitive damages to teach a duty of care. We would allow a jury to impose substantial punitive damages in order to discourage bad acts.

The Court upheld the punitive damage award based upon evidence that the defendant engaged in a pattern of malicious and fraudulent behavior in an attempt to deprive the plaintiff of royalties.

The first case in which the Supreme Court invalidated on substantive grounds a punitive damage award under the Due Process Clause was *BMW v. Gore* (S.Ct.1996). The case involved a claim against an automobile manufacturer for failure to disclose that a new car had been repainted prior to delivery. The manufacturer had a policy of not disclosing repairs if they did not exceed three percent of the value. The Alabama jury awarded the plaintiff $4,000 in compensatory damages and $4 million in punitive damages. The Alabama Supreme Court concluded that the punitive damage award was excessive and reduced the award to $2 million.

The Court held in *Gore* that the punitive damage award violated due process because it was so grossly excessive that the defendant lacked fair notice that it would be imposed. The Court further approved several "guideposts" to evaluate the constitutionality of punitive damage awards. Those factors are: (1) the degree of reprehensibility of the person's conduct; (2) the reasonableness of the ratio between the harm or potential harm suffered by the victim and his punitive damage award; and (3) the comparison of the punitive damage award and the civil or criminal penalties authorized or imposed in comparable cases. The Court noted that this list is not exhaustive. Some courts, for example, have also considered the wealth of the defendant, the profit incentive associated with the wrongful conduct, and the plaintiff's litigation costs in the evaluation of the reasonableness of punitive awards.

In addition to these substantive safeguards, procedural safeguards are necessary to satisfy due process. The Supreme Court held in *Honda Motor Co., Ltd. v. Oberg* (S.Ct.1994) that the Due Process Clause requires meaningful judicial review of such verdicts to prevent the arbitrary deprivation of property through an excessive award. The Court has also held that an appellate court should review de novo a district court's evaluation of whether a punitive damage award was unconstitutionally excessive. Cooper Industries v. Leatherman Tool Group (S.Ct.2001).

(F) Legislative Reform

Increasing numbers of state legislatures have enacted statutes that regulate the availability and amount of punitive damages. Some of the most common measures include: heightening the burden of proof above the traditional preponderance of the evidence, bifurcating the proceedings involving punitive awards and compensatory damages, and placing ceilings on awards.

Some state statutory schemes have been creative in their attempts to deal with the issues. Georgia, for example, has addressed the problem of multiple punitive damage awards for the same conduct in at least one circumstance. Their rule now permits only one plaintiff to recover a punitive damage award from a defendant for any act or omission if the plaintiff's cause of action is a product liability case. Some other jurisdictions have enacted "extraction statutes" that require some portion of a punitive recovery be directed to the state. The policy justification is that the allocation of funds to the public treasury for various purposes, such as to supplement education, advances the public interest in punishing and deterring conduct that offends social norms.

Congress has considered, but not as yet enacted, proposals for federal legislation to control punitive damages. Proposed legislation has sought to reduce or eliminate multiple punitive damage awards. The primary concern of Congress in this area has been the award of punitive damages in product liability cases with numerous victims.

Chapter 16

UNJUST ENRICHMENT ~ Focus

(A) The Unjust Enrichment Concept

The underlying policy of restitution is to prevent the unjust enrichment of a party who has received a benefit that, in equity and good conscience, should not be retained. Restitution cuts across many areas of law and may arise as a remedial option in numerous situations. Entitlement does not hinge upon a showing of wrongful conduct on the part of the defendant, although usually such conduct is present. Rather, the central inquiry is whether the claimant is rightfully entitled to the restoration of certain benefits which unjustly enrich the defendant.

After issues of entitlement, the second question in restitution is the measurement of the benefit. The restitutionary measure focuses on the gain unjustly retained by the defendant rather than the loss to the plaintiff. The difference in focus between restitution and compensatory damages often produces different dollar amounts. Claimants frequently have a choice of actions and can pursue the highest possible recovery.

(B) Benefits Acquired by Mistake

Restitution is a useful remedial option when one or both parties to a contract have made a mistaken assumption about something material to the contract. Mistake alone does not invalidate an otherwise valid agreement because contract law has a strong policy favoring the finality and the integrity of the bargain. Consequently, the standards for setting aside agreements are stringent and the existence of a mistake does not constitute a breach of contract giving rise to compensatory damages.

Rather, certain types of mistakes can support legal or equitable remedies, such as reformation or rescission and restitution. The substantive question for purposes of restitution is simply whether the retention of certain benefits by the defendant would be unjust. Mistake, for purposes of avoidance, must be distinguished from doctrines like ambiguity or failed predictions of future market conditions.

The Restatement (Second) of Contracts § 151 defines "mistake" as a "belief that is not in accord with the facts." Not all mistaken beliefs justify contract avoidance, however. Instead, the mistake must be considered "material" and pertain to a "basic assumption on which the contract was made." *See* Restatement (Second) of Contracts Contracts § § 152, 153. The reason for those requirements is that they affect the very nature of the bargained-for exchange, and if erroneous, may contravene the intentions of the parties in assuming risks and obligations under the agreement. The party seeking relief must not be deemed to bear the risk of the mistake either according to the terms of the agreement or as allocated by the court. *See* Restatement (Second) of Contracts § 154.

A mistake that may justify some remedy can occur during formation, integration or performance of the contract. The nature of the appropriate remedy will vary depending upon when the mistake occurred and whether it is classified as mutual or unilateral. Courts have allowed avoidance for unilateral mistake only in very limited circumstances. The mistaken party must further demonstrate either that the enforcement of the contract would be unconscionable or that the other party had reason to know of the mistake or was at fault in causing it. *See* Restatement (Second) of Contracts § 153.

An illustration of a mutual mistake in the formation of a contract is when both parties have an erroneous belief that the subject matter of the contract is in existence when in fact it has been destroyed. Such a mutual mistake in contract formation may justify an order of rescission and restitution of benefits conferred if the mistake materially affects the basic assumptions of the parties. The remaining rights and duties of the parties are terminated without obligation or consequence.

A mistake in integration of the agreement may justify the equitable remedy of reformation. This equitable device simply corrects the error to correspond to the true intentions of the parties, but the contract itself remains intact.

Finally, a mistake by one party during the course of performance of a contract may give rise to a claim for restitution from the holder of the benefit who may be otherwise unjustly enriched. Some jurisdictions permit restitution when a party mistakenly pays the debt of another under circumstances not amounting to a gift or volunteer payment.

(C) Misrepresentation and Fraud

Where benefits are conferred by an agreement that was induced by fraud or misrepresentation, the injured party may have a claim for damages or restitution. There are several significant differences in these remedies. The substantive criteria for establishing fraud under common law tort or contract principles requires a showing of wrongful intent, for example. In contrast, a claim for restitution requires consideration if benefits would be unjustly retained.

The measure of recovery also may differ markedly. Courts can typically use two alternative methods to measure damages for fraud, both of which compensate for the plaintiff's actual loss. The "out of pocket" approach allows the difference between the price paid and the value actually received. For example, if the seller of a house fraudulently represents that a leaky roof was recently repaired, the buyer may recover the difference between the contract price and the value of the defective house. The benefit of the bargain method calculates damages by the difference between the value of the house as received compared with the value of the property as represented.

Another significant difference between a fraud claim and restitution may be the availability of attorneys' fees for contract-based actions. Attorneys' fees may be available either by state statute or pursuant to the agreement but generally will not be awarded for claims sounding in tort. A restitutionary remedy, such as quasi-contract, could be classified under a jurisdiction's contract claims and allow fee-shifting. Also, punitive damages could potentially be available for a tort claim of fraudulent inducement but generally is not awarded in equity via restitution.

(D) Quantum Meruit — False

Restitution at law may provide an appropriate remedy to restore benefits acquired pursuant to a failed or unenforceable agreement. Classic illustrations include contracts in violation of the Statute of Frauds or contracts entered into by a party without authority or lacking capacity. Some contracts may be deemed unenforceable at inception. Others become so due to impossibility of performance, or because the defendant materially breaches and the plaintiff elects to treat the contract as ended.

Various restitutionary devices address the goal of disgorging the unjust enrichment of benefits that were originally conferred by agreement. Rescission and restitution are traditional equitable remedies available both for the breach of a contract and disgorging benefits originally bestowed under an unenforceable agreement. When courts will order restitution by defendants in such cases, they also require plaintiffs to restore any benefits received pursuant to the agreement. The principle of making restitution mutually equitable is reflected by the maxim, "He who seeks equity must do equity."

One important restitutionary tool to achieve restitution of benefits pursuant to an unenforceable agreement is called quantum meruit. The term literally means "as much as he deserves", and comes from the historical "common counts" that functioned as quasi-contracts. The remedy is not a true contract at all in the same sense as an express or implied-in-fact bargained for exchange. Rather, a quasi-contract is a fiction implied by law by the court to achieve a certain result. The reason why courts refer to such arrangements as "quasi" contracts is that it describes the relationship assigned by a court imposing a duty of restoring benefits to the rightful owner. In contrast with express contracts where the intent of the parties guides and informs the determination of compensatory damages for breach, a quasi-contract is not based on adhering to such intentions nor giving the benefit of the bargain. Instead, the purpose is to provide a restitutionary vehicle to accomplish the conveyance of benefits to the claimant and preventing the unjust enrichment of the defendant.

Although jurisdictions vary somewhat in their formulation, the basic requirements for establishing quantum meruit are: (1) valuable materials or services were rendered by the plaintiff, (2) the services were conferred for the benefit of the person sought to be charged, (3) the defendant accepted and enjoyed the benefits, and (4) the circumstances demonstrate that the plaintiff had a reasonable expectation of being compensated by the defendant for the benefits conferred. The measure of recovery is the reasonable value of the materials or services.

Quantum meruit is not available as an alternative remedy where performance under a valid contract has been completed and all that remains is the payment of the contract price. When only the contract amount remains unpaid, a plaintiff may sue for the debt with the remedy indebitatus assumpsit. Once performance is complete, the contract price is a liquidated debt.

In contrast, quantum meruit may be available where a contract has only partially been completed or where the agreement is "divisible" or severable. The aggrieved party may sue for the debt owed for the divisible performance but may not rescind the entire contract and sue in quantum meruit for the value of the services independent of the contract price.

(E) Constructive Trusts and Equitable Liens

The constructive trust is an important equitable restitutionary remedy designed to prevent unjust enrichment by effectuating the transfer of property to the claimant asserting equitable title. The trust characterization actually describes a fictional construct which serves to achieve a desired method and result of conveying the subject property. As such, it is created implicitly by a court, and is therefore distinguishable from express trust arrangements which are created by the parties themselves.

The "constructive" aspect of the equitable trust means that it operates generally like an express trust in the functional relationship of the parties where the trust *res* is held by the trustee for the beneficiary. The defendant-trustee is not a fiduciary, however, in the same manner as other trust agreements, but rather is just the holder of the property who is charged by the court with the duty to effect conveyance to the claimant, as beneficiary. The equitable remedy is distinguishable, though, because it is not based on an agreement of the parties, and even may be established contrary to the objectives of one of the parties.

A close counterpart to the equitable constructive trust is the quasi-contract, which is implied in law. Neither are predicated on carrying out the intentions of the parties, as in an implied-in-fact or express contract, but are established by the court to accomplish the restitutionary objective of restoring property to the rightful owner. An important difference between the restitutionary remedy in equity is that it is imposed upon specifically identifiable property to which the claimant has established a superior equitable title, while the quasi-contract claim is directed against the general assets of the defendant. A major benefit of the constructive trust, then, is that the party may obtain property *in specie* rather than having to compete with other general creditors of the defendant for finding assets to satisfy their claims.

An equitable lien is a close cousin to the more commonly used constructive trust. The lien may be created either from an express agreement between parties that somehow fails to comply with the requirements for common law liens, yet may still enforceable in equity to carry out the express or implied intentions of the parties. The more typical illustration of an equitable lien, though, is to serve as an alternative restitutionary remedy in situations where a constructive trust may be inappropriate. For example, since a constructive trust provides a conveyance *in specie* of the property to the beneficiary of the trust, it assumes that appropriate title can be delivered. In situations where property cannot be fully conveyed, such as where converted assets have been commingled with other property previously owned by a wrongdoer, a constructive trust of the whole would result in a windfall or forfeiture to the beneficiary. An equitable lien, though, could be imposed against the property to the extent necessary to prevent unjust enrichment.

The lien and constructive trust, as equitable restitutionary devices, share certain commonalities but also have important differences both in function and in practice. Since they sound in equity, both entitlement and measurement are discretionary with the court and are designed to prevent unjust enrichment. They are both directed against specifically traced real or personal property, as opposed to the general assets of the party sought to be charged.

There is a broad range of situations that justify imposition of these remedies, including wrongdoing by embezzlement, fraud, and sometimes conversion, as well as mistaken payment or improvement of property. Both remedies require a tracing of property, dispense with jury trial, are not effective against bona fide purchasers for value, and are enforceable with the contempt power of courts. Although a split of authority exists regarding whether the remedies should require a showing of inadequacy of legal remedies, the modern trend appears to favor less emphasis on legal remedial alternatives than would be ordinarily required for issuance of injunctive relief.

There are important differences between these two remedies. Most notably, the constructive trust involves conveyance of title, while the lien operates as a charge or encumbrance against specific property. The trust is more advantageous when the defendant is insolvent because the subject titled property is restored to the rightful owner. The lien-holder does gain a priority over general creditors with respect to the specified property, but still must obtain a further foreclosure order to satisfy the claim. The trust allows the beneficiary to obtain increases in value of the traced assets, such as where embezzled funds are invested in a profitable venture. The lien is limited to a sum certain. Apart from the issue of title, an equitable lien may be more advantageous when the property charged has declined in value. In that situation the holder can obtain a security interest in that property coupled with a deficiency money judgment against the debtor for the balance owed.

The measure of the remedy is governed by considerations of equitable restitution generally, and will seek to prevent unjust enrichment by disgorging the benefits enjoyed by the defendant. For example, where improvements are made to realty, the court may grant an equitable lien for the enhanced value of the premises. If the improvements did not increase the market value of the property, a court may award the reasonable value of the labor or materials furnished by the party seeking restitution. The claimant will not receive a forfeiture, however, nor double recovery, even in circumstances where the defendant acted in bad faith. Restitution is not punitive but seeks simply to disgorge benefits unjustly held and to restore them to the rightful owner.

(F) Waiver of Tort and Suit in Assumpsit

Waiver of tort and suit in assumpsit is a legal restitutionary device that disgorges unjust enrichment through quasi-contracts. Although the parties have no contract between them, the common law will imply one that requires a defendant to return unjust enrichment to a plaintiff who should more rightfully retain it. It applies as an alternative remedy to conversion and some jurisdictions permit use of the theory for profits gained from trespass. It can also apply when tortious behavior results in a saving to the defendant that should not be retained. Olwell v. Nye & Nissen (Wash.1946).

This type of restitution was accomplished historically by allowing a plaintiff to use one of the old contract writs even in the absence of an express or implied contract. The writ of "money had and received" was thus used for this quasi-contract in order to create a fictional agency between the wrongdoer who converted property and its owner. As an agent, the wrongdoer was then obliged to repay the owner any proceeds from the resale of that property. Modern law has retained this fiction even though it is no longer necessary to use writs.

This remedy is superior to compensatory damages for conversion in the situation where the defendant has resold the property for a price greater than its fair market value. It is also a useful remedy in any conversion situation if the statute of limitations has expired on the tort. The action of waiving the tort and suing in assumpsit transforms the tort claim into a contract claim. The statute of limitations for contract is typically many years longer than for tort.

Some jurisdictions have expanded this remedy to create a fictional sale between an owner and the defendant who converted property. The quasi-contract theory then is for an implied contract of sale between these parties for purchase of the converted item at its fair market value. Historically this result was accomplished by use of the writ for "goods sold and delivered." Felder v. Reeth (9th Cir.1929). This remedy produces the same dollar recovery as a conversion action, but has the advantage of extending the statute of limitations because the action is now in contract. *See* H. Russell Taylor's Fire Prevention Service, Inc. v. Coca Cola Bottling Corp. (Cal.App.1979).

Chapter 17

LIMITS ON RESTITUTIONARY REMEDIES

(A) Volunteers

A general rule in restitution is that someone who confers an unsolicited benefit to another without their knowledge or consent cannot claim that the benefit is unjust enrichment. *See* Restatement of Restitution § 2. The party seeking restitution is often characterized as a "volunteer" or an "officious intermeddler." The description does not refer to wrongdoing or tortious behavior, but refers to the character of the action. The action is a voluntary one when the goods or services are rendered without invitation and when the recipient lacks a choice in their acceptance.

The rule against recovery for volunteers is based on two policy considerations. First, if the law permitted compensation for unwanted interference with another's property, it would create an incentive for intermeddling with the interests of others. Second, courts have consistently recognized that public policy supports the freedom of persons to choose the circumstances and conditions upon which they enter into transactions.

A common illustration of officious intermeddling is where a volunteer makes unsolicited improvements on another's land and then demands payment. The improvements may enhance the value of the land, such as if a barn were painted or a fence erected, but the landowner is not held legally accountable for the benefits because the volunteer acted without knowledge or consent of the owner. The principle of denying restitution to officious intermeddlers applies broadly and includes providing services, making improvements to land, transferring property, or paying debts.

The law does recognize some limited situations in which public policy justifies awarding restitution even where knowledge or consent of the volunteered services is lacking. In these situations the conduct of the actor is not inappropriate or "officious" but rather may be furthering an important public interest. For example, restitution may be given for furnishing necessaries to a minor child. A parent who has a legal duty of care for the child may be held liable for the benefits conferred even if provided without their knowledge or consent. The concept of "necessaries" encompasses items like food, clothing, or medicine which would be essential for the preservation and enjoyment of life. *See* Restatement of Restitution, comment d, section 113. The person seeking restitution must have furnished the goods or services with an expectation of compensation and not gratuitously or pursuant to a contractual arrangement. The public policy favoring restitution is to promote protection of minors and to encourage diligence of persons responsible for their welfare. The measure of recovery generally is based upon the market value of the goods or services.

Another exception is emergency situations where action is necessary to prevent serious personal harm or suffering. *See* Restatement of Restitution § 114(b). The public interest in preserving life or health outweighs the traditional judicial disinclination to give restitution for unsolicited benefits. The party seeking restitution must have an expectation of payment at the time the services were rendered. The rule recognizes that some persons who need emergency services may not be in a position to give consent because of age or infirmity yet presumptively would do so willingly if competent. An illustration is where a person is unconscious following an accident and is subsequently treated by a Good Samaritan physician who stops and renders life-saving medical treatment.

In contrast, services volunteered to preserve someone else's property are gratuitous acts of kindness that may create a moral obligation of payment but not a legal one. This philosophy was articulated in a well-known early case, *Bartholomew v. Jackson* (N.Y.1922). The opinion observed: ''If a man humanely bestows his labor, and even risks his life, in voluntarily aiding to preserve his neighbor's house from destruction by fire, the law considers the service rendered as gratuitous, and it therefore forms no ground of action.''

Despite judicial reluctance to compensate voluntary preservation of personal property, recovery is permitted in limited situations. The standards for entitlement, though, are considerably higher than where providing necessary assistance to protect a person's health and safety. The requirements include an intent to charge for the services rendered and lack of an opportunity to communicate with the owner. Further, the actions must be necessary for protection of the property, and the owner must choose to accept the benefit. *See* Restatement § 117. Restitution is measured by the reasonable value of the services necessary to preserve the property. The rationale for stricter standards for restitution in this circumstance is the paramount value of human life over property interests.

Restitution may be awarded when benefits are conferred upon another by mistake. For example, a bank error accidentally crediting the wrong account with funds is not voluntarily bestowing a benefit. A party who mistakenly discharges a financial obligation of another also is not considered an officious intermeddler because they acted without any intent to confer a benefit upon a third party. Some jurisdictions are reluctant to permit a substitution of creditors, however, and refuse restitution on that grounds.

In situations involving mistaken improvements to land, courts may base recovery in restitution on whether the improvements are fixtures or capable of removal. Where the landowner has a choice of accepting the benefit, such as where a fence or shed could be removed, restitution is allowed when the owner retains the improvement. If the improvement cannot be severed, such as a coat of paint on a barn, the court will consider the equities and balance the hardships in deciding both entitlement and measurement in restitution. The cases are not without difficulty, however. If restitution is given, the landowner still bears responsibility of paying for something that was not bargained for and may actually interfere with other potential uses of the land. If denied, the mistaken improver confers a benefit with no countervailing compensation. Along with these competing considerations, other factors include the knowledge of the parties and the extent of the benefit conferred. The measure of any recovery is typically the lesser of the increase in value of the property or the value of labor and materials used in making the improvements. See Restatement of Restitution § 42.

(B) Tracing

A principal requirement for imposing a constructive trust or equitable lien is that the claimant must trace the sequence of property transactions or exchanges into its present form. The use of tracing to achieve equitable restitution has a long history, originating in suits against trustees and fiduciaries, but also involving cases of fraud, conversion, mistake or breach of contract. *See* Palmer on Restitution § 2.14. The restitutionary remedy may further allow the rightful owner to seek recourse either from the wrongdoer, an innocent donee, gratuitous transferee, holders of property received by mistake, or possibly in the hands of a third party subsequent transferee.

The claimant bears the burden of establishing the trail of exchanged or transferred property but may do so through unlimited transactions. The inability to trace exchanged property will defeat entitlement to equitable restitution even though the claimant still retains full legal remedies. The loss of the equitable remedy may be very significant, however. With a constructive trust, for example, a claimant may be able to recover traced property *in specie* and thus benefit from an increase in value of the property. An equitable lien does not capture any increased value, but like the constructive trust, it offers priority over general unsecured creditors. This advantage is particularly significant when the wrongdoer is insolvent.

Another advantage of equitable restitution is to enable the claimant to reach certain property that would otherwise be unavailable to satisfy a claim at law. For example, if a wrongdoer misappropriates funds and uses the proceeds to acquire a homestead property, it would be considered exempt from a judgment creditor yet potentially available for imposing an equitable lien. The principles of equity to prevent unjust enrichment may outweigh the statutory policy of a homestead exemption. This result depends upon the ability of the claimant to trace the embezzled funds into that particular property.

When claimants trace property to funds used to make improvements upon land or chattels already owned by another, they may be entitled to either a common law or statutory lien or an equitable lien. A constructive trust is not available, however, because the conveyance of the entire property would result in a windfall to the claimant and exceed the objective of preventing unjust enrichment.

A claimant's ability to trace and recover specific assets through equitable restitution is particularly significant where the wrongdoer is insolvent. The Restatement of Restitution allows a claimant to reach traced property and enforce specific restitution even against an insolvent wrongdoer. It requires tracing of the legal or equitable interest. *See* section 202, comment e. Others criticize this position as unduly favoring claimants at the expense of other general creditors.

Equitable restitution may reach not only traced property but also its product. For example, if a wrongdoer purchases stock with embezzled funds, a constructive trust may be used to convey the stock itself as well as any dividends received from the stock shares. Some courts limit recovery of profits to situations involving a showing of moral blame or "conscious wrongdoing," and limit the liability of an innocent converter to the value of the property held.

A difficult tracing problem arises when a person wrongfully commingles property belonging to another with personal assets, such as depositing embezzled funds in the wrongdoer's pre-existing bank account. Although the misappropriated money has lost its separate identity in the commingled account, courts will impose an equitable lien on the account to allow restitution of the amount which rightfully belongs to the plaintiff. The claimant would be unjustly enriched if the court granted restitution of the entire fund; conversely, a wrongdoer should not be able to foreclose restitution simply by the act of commingling funds. In situations involving a series of deposits and withdrawals, the burden of tracing and identifying specific funds becomes factually impossible. As a result, different approaches have been created to liberalize the tracing requirement so as not to unfairly provide a wrongdoer with a windfall or safe haven simply because they commingled misappropriated funds.

In an early English decision known as *Clayton's Case, Devaynes v. Noble* (1816), the court ruled that the first money put into an account would be presumed the first money withdrawn. The rule was predicated on the idea that the claimant would probably benefit by being able to reach the funds remaining in an account because the wrongdoer's funds would have been withdrawn and dissipated first. Under this "first in, first out" approach, the claimant's recovery would depend upon the fortuity of the timing of when the various funds and their product were either dissipated or profitably invested.

A later English decision, *In re Hallett's Estate* (1879) modified the rule in *Clayton's Case* by holding that the first withdrawals from a commingled fund would be treated presumptively as belonging to the wrongdoer, leaving the remaining funds available to imposition of the claimant's equitable interest. Known as the rule of Jessel's Bag, referring to a member of the court, Sir George Jessel, this method would often benefit the claimant because typically the first moneys withdrawn by a wrongdoer from a commingled fund would be dissipated. The money left in the account would be available for satisfying equitable claims. A further refinement of the tracing fictions in *In re Oatway* (Ch.Div.1903) simply gives the claimant the choice between following the withdrawn funds or those remaining in an account, reasoning that the order of priority of deposits and withdrawals should be immaterial.

The Restatement of Restitution § 211 rejects all the tracing fictions and gives the claimant an equitable lien in the commingled fund and its traceable product. Under the Restatement approach, the sequence or timing of deposits and withdrawals does not dictate the choice of remedy as that is often fortuitous. In cases involving "conscious wrongdoing", the Restatement allows the claimant an option of a proportionate share both of the remaining funds and the property withdrawn. *See generally* Palmer, The Law of Restitution § 2.17 (1978). The rules apply uniformly irrespective of whether the funds are physically commingled, deposited in an existing bank account, or used to pay some premiums upon a life insurance policy.

Additional tracing issues occur when a wrongdoer makes withdrawals from a commingled account, dissipates those funds, and then later makes additional deposits of personal funds into the same account. Should the deposits be treated as a restoration of the claimant's money or instead as belonging to the wrongdoer? The Restatement of Restitution position is that the claimant's equitable interest in the fund is limited to the lowest intermediate balance of the account. *See* Restatement of Restitution § 212. The claimant can reach the additional funds only by showing that the wrongdoer made the deposits intending to make restitution.

(C) Bona Fide Purchaser

A bona fide purchaser is a party who acts in good faith and pays value for legal title to property without notice of an outstanding equitable interest. The law protects a bona fide purchaser against prior equitable claims. This rule protecting certain transferees is based on several policies. A primary justification is to ensure certainty and to protect the integrity of commercial transactions. In short, the buyer who acts in good faith and without actual or constructive knowledge of equitable interests is effectively given the legal assurance that the title obtained will be honored. Another rationale underlying the bona fide purchaser doctrine is that legal title historically has been considered superior to equitable title. Finally, the doctrine is consistent with the view that, as between two innocent parties, the loss should not fall on the one who paid value.

Several requirements must be met in order to claim bona fide purchaser status: the party must acquire legal title, for value, and without notice of prior equitable interests. The lack of any element will suffice to defeat the protected status. The defense applies to virtually any type of property rights, including realty, personalty, and negotiable instruments. The application of the defense will vary, however, depending on the nature of the property interest at stake and the overlay of various statutes. For example, the recording statutes pertaining to real property impose a filing of the deed or mortgage in a central location which itself serves as constructive notice to the world of that interest. The Uniform Commercial Code contains various provisions that affect the bona fide purchaser rules, such as sections 2–402 and 1–201(44) regarding what constitutes paying "value."

Consider the following illustration: A wrongfully transfers legal title to property held in trust to B, who has no notice that the transfer violates the trust agreement nor of the interest of the true beneficiary, C. If B has paid value for the property, however, B would be protected as a bona fide purchaser against the equitable interest asserted by the beneficiary in the trust *res*. C could maintain an action for fraud or breach of the trust agreement against A, but could not seek reconveyance from B through equitable restitution. On the other hand, if B did not pay value, such as if B were classified as an innocent donee, then C would prevail because all of the required elements of the bona fide purchaser defense were not met.

The notice that can defeat bona fide purchaser status can be actual or constructive. Constructive notice is satisfied when a deed, will, mortgage, or other instrument has been duly recorded in a public office under state law recording statutes. *See* Restatement of Restitution § 174 comment b. Thus, a purchaser of real estate is given a safe harbor of protection by reliance on recorded titles, and will ordinarily not be subordinated to unrecorded equities of which the purchaser has no actual or constructive knowledge.

Constructive notice may arise in other ways as well. A principal may be charged with the knowledge of an agent acquired during the agency relationship. Also, notice may be imputed to a transferee in situations where the prior equitable claim would have been discovered by the exercise of reasonable due diligence. Even a fact such as a very low purchase price of property may suffice to place the potential buyer on notice that the property has an outstanding equitable claim against it.

The U.C.C. provides a greater latitude to a holder of negotiable instruments, who will take free of equitable claims if value was paid in good faith even where the holder failed to satisfy a duty of objective due diligence to discover a fraud. *See* U.C.C. §§ 1–201(19)(25); 3–304; 8–304. The rationale for giving heightened protection to the holder of negotiable instruments is to promote certainty in commercial transactions.

A transferee must also give "value" for the acquired property in order to receive bona fide purchaser status. The concept of sufficient value is reasonably flexible, based on the nature of the property at issue. Mathematical precision is not required. A person receiving property gratuitously will not meet the standard, and a very low purchase price may also fail as "value." *See* Restatement of Restitution § 173 comment b. The U.C.C. § 1–201(44) defines value as "any consideration sufficient to support a simple contract." The satisfaction of an antecedent debt constitutes giving value sufficient to cut off the beneficial interest in a constructive trust but not against the beneficiary of an express trust. A person receiving property as security for or in satisfaction of a pre-existing obligation is generally considered a purchaser for value under the modern trend.

In re Marriage of Allen (Colo.1986) illustrates the requirement that a bona fide purchaser must have given value for the property. In that case a husband used embezzled funds to make home improvements and then the property interest was included in a divorce settlement agreement. The employer traced the proceeds to a portion of the wife's share of the settlement arrangement, and sought a constructive trust to convey the misappropriated assets. Although the wife was not charged with notice of the embezzlement, she was not accorded bona fide purchaser status. The court reasoned that she did not give value for the property. As an innocent donee or gratuitous transferee of the property, she did not give value.

A transferee, in addition to giving value and acquiring property without notice of equitable claims, must obtain legal title rather than equitable title in order to prevail as a bona fide purchaser over the competing equitable interests. A bona fide purchaser's rights are superior to prior equitable interests. In contrast, a judgment creditor possessing a statutory lien on property is not accorded the same priority status over previous equitable claims even though the creditor had no notice of such equitable interest. Restatement (First) of Restitution § 173 cmt. j.(1937).

(D) Change in Position

Another defense to restitution is known as "change in position." It provides that a court of equity may exercise its discretion to withhold or limit restitution if the order would result in a substantial hardship due to changed circumstances of the defendant. The defense has been applied sparingly because the standard for its application is especially rigorous. Because this defense defeats an otherwise meritorious claim for restitution, the change in the defendant's position must be compelling.

This defense reflects the traditional discretion of a court of equity to fashion its orders based upon the relative hardships of the affected parties. Consequently, although one party has held or enjoyed a benefit that ordinarily may justify disgorgement, subsequent events may influence the willingness of a court to order restitution. For example, if goods are destroyed by fire, without tortious conduct or fault by the holder, a court may decide not to require restitution. A common example of the change of position defense is where a person mistakenly delivers goods to another and then the goods are lost or destroyed without the fault of the recipient. Assuming that the holder of the mistakenly delivered property did not have a duty of care toward the property or its rightful owner, the change in position defense can apply.

The application of the defense requires an inquiry into the degree of hardship and the materiality of the change in position. The court also will examine the defendant's own conduct toward the property before asserting the defense. If the defendant committed a tort or was substantially more at fault than the claimant, the defense is unavailable. The defendant must show that the change in circumstances occurred prior to learning the relevant facts and before there was an opportunity to make restitution. Finally, the nature of the loss or destruction of the property is relevant. If the recipient has exercised reasonable reliance or if a long period of time has elapsed since acquiring the property interest, they may be given more latitude in asserting the defense.

An interesting example of these principles at work is *Alexander Hamilton Life Ins. Co. v. Lewis* (Ky.1977). In that case the plaintiff insurance company had paid proceeds on a life insurance policy to the defendant beneficiaries on the mutually mistaken believe that the insured was deceased. The defendants had not committed wrongdoing and had spent the funds prior to receiving notice of the true status of the insured. The recipients had expended the funds for ordinary living expenses, home improvements, medical expenses and for purchase of an automobile. The court did not accept the change in position defense and ordered equitable restitution of the funds. The court reasoned that the defense did not apply to prevent restoration of the mistakenly paid funds because of the balance of respective hardships of the parties and the types of expenses incurred. Most jurisdictions agree that dissipation of funds in normal living expenses does not amount to a change in position that discharges an obligation to repay.

Courts interpret the defense of change is position in a manner consistent with the general principles underlying equitable restitution. Someone who acquires property without fault has a duty to restore it to its owner unless the property has been a gift or otherwise acquired under circumstances that do not make it unjust to retain. The duty of restitution does not arise until the recipient learns the facts that make restitution appropriate. Therefore, if the goods are consumed, lost, stolen, transferred or destroyed in the interim, their duty of restitution is limited to the extent of the benefit enjoyed.

Chapter 18

JURY TRIALS

(A) Substantive Equity

Historically, the courts of equity took two types of cases. One was cases where the remedy at law was inadequate. This basis was explored through the inadequacy rule covered in chapters 3 and 4. The second type was cases of substantive equity. Cases involving trusts, mortgages, and shareholder derivative actions were a matter of substantive equity rather than remedial equity because only equity recognized these claims. The courts at law had no effective way of handling these substantive claims, so equity devised means of dealing with these areas. Thus, any case concerning these substantive matters came under equitable jurisdiction regardless of the type of remedy sought in these claims.

Most states retain the rule that there is no right to a jury trial for a claim brought in equity. This rule applies to substantive equity as well as remedial equity. Therefore, if a shareholder derivative action is tried in state court, there is no right to a jury trial in most states. It does not matter if the complaint seeks remedies that are legal ones, such as damages for alleged fraud by the company's officers. Unlike remedial equity, it is the nature of the claim that makes such a case an equitable one.

The Supreme Court has changed that rule for cases of substantive equity brought in federal court. In *Ross v. Bernhard* (S.Ct.1970) the Court addressed whether shareholders were entitled to a jury trial in a derivative suit under the federal guarantee of a right to a jury trial embodied in the Seventh Amendment. The problem was how to reconcile the historical development of substantive equity with the commands of the Seventh Amendment which provides for a right to jury trial in matters "at law." The Court decided to ignore the "historical accident" of substantive equity and to focus instead upon the legal or equitable nature of the remedy sought in the underlying claim. Therefore, because the plaintiffs in *Ross* sought damages, there was a right to a jury trial.

The Court's conclusion in *Ross* applies only to federal jury trial rights because the Seventh Amendment does not apply to the states. Some states have been persuaded by the Supreme Court's analysis and have interpreted their own state Constitutional guarantees in the same manner. Most states have not followed the Supreme Court's approach and have retained the rule that claims in substantive equity do not support a right to a jury trial.

(B) Equitable Clean–Up

The merger of law and equity in the twentieth century brought the reform that mixed claims of law and equity could be brought in one claim and before one judge. The merger was procedural only, and did not change the substantive differences between law and equity.

When a plaintiff brings a purely legal claim to a merged court, there is a right to a jury trial. Therefore, a claim seeking damages for breach of contract supports a right to a jury trial in the merged court. There is no such right when the claim is purely equitable, such as one for specific performance.

Problems arise when the plaintiff brings a mixed claim that seeks both legal and equitable relief, or when a plaintiff brings one type of claim and the defendant counterclaims with a different type. Historically, courts handled this situation with the doctrine called "equitable clean up." Under this doctrine, if a case is primarily equitable in nature, a judge can resolve the legal issues without a jury. For example, consider a nuisance claim where a plaintiff seeks an injunction to prevent future loss as well as damages for past losses. If the injunction issue predominates, then the trial judge can decide the equitable remedy issues and then decide the damages issues. The parties have no right to a jury trial because the judge can "clean up" the remaining legal issues after deciding the equitable ones.

Most states still follow the clean-up doctrine. The Supreme Court has rejected this approach for federal courts, however, as an interpretation of the Seventh Amendment. This Constitutional guarantee to a right to a jury trial in matters "at law" has never been applied to the states, so its interpretation affects only federal procedure. The Supreme Court held in *Dairy Queen, Inc. v. Wood* (S.Ct.1962) that the clean-up doctrine violates the Seventh Amendment right to a jury trial in cases at law. Consequently, a federal court must first try any legal issues before a jury, unless the parties waive that right. After the determination of the legal issues, the judge may then resolve any equitable issues in a manner not inconsistent with the verdict.

Chapter 19

ATTORNEYS' FEES

Attorneys' fees are traditionally not awarded to the prevailing party in litigation absent statute, contract, or satisfying certain equitable exceptions. This is the "American Rule" that each party bears its own costs of litigation. It is distinguished from the English approach that allows for recovery of such fees. The English practice is that the winning party recovers litigation expenses as a matter of course from the losing party. Such litigation expenses include attorneys' fees, and the rule applies equally to prevailing plaintiffs and defendants. *See* generally McCormick, Damages § 60 (1935).

The American Rule is supported by several policy considerations. The primary justification for refusing attorneys' fees to the winning party is to avoid penalizing a party for its reasonable claim or defense. The party that loses on the merits is not a "wrongdoer," and to impose fees may discourage the legitimate use of the court system. A handful of courts have also justified the rule by pointing to the potential difficulties and burden of proving what constitutes a reasonable fee.

The American Rule has been sharply criticized on several grounds as well. One objection is that the failure to reimburse litigation expenses to a successful parties prevents them from being "made whole" even after winning the case. Further, if the only relief granted is an injunction, no pool of damages would be available to defray litigation costs. A different line of objection to the rule is that it encourages litigation by not penalizing losers.

The American Rule is the default rule in litigation, but a number of exceptions also have been recognized. The exceptions come from agreement, policy, and statute. Some reflect dissatisfaction with the potential inequity in bearing litigation costs. Other exceptions are designed to encourage certain types of litigation in the public interest.

(A) The Contract Exception

One major exception to the American Rule is that parties may stipulate by contract to the payment of attorneys' fees when a non-breaching party must enforce the agreement. Such contractual fee-shifting provisions are generally upheld provided they are not unconscionable. Attorneys' fee provisions are commonly included in commercial agreements, such as bank loans and leases. Also, some states have enacted statutes that provide for the award of attorneys' fees to secure compensation for breach of contract.

(B) Equitable Exceptions

(1) Bad Faith Litigation

A court has inherent equitable power to award reasonable attorney fees to the prevailing party when the losing party has acted in acted in "bad faith, vexatiously, wantonly, or for oppressive reasons" in the conduct of the litigation. Chambers v. NASCO, Inc. (S.Ct.1991). In *Chambers*, the buyer of a television station sought to compel completion of the transaction, but the seller engaged in a series of delay and obstruction tactics to prevent enforcement of the court's orders. The Supreme Court upheld the fee award imposed by the district court based upon the bad faith exception to the American Rule. The Court observed that the award of fees for bad faith litigation serves the dual purpose of vindicating the integrity of the court and making the prevailing party whole for expenses caused by the opponent's conduct. The Court further found that the bad faith equity exception could be used even if other rules also provided sanctions. Finally, the opinion approved the award of fees by federal courts sitting in diversity even when the applicable state law did not recognize the bad faith exception to the American Rule.

The standard of bad faith under this rule requires more than simply showing that the claim or defense had a weak foundation. Instead, the claim must have been frivolous or without merit.

(2) Common Fund

Another exception to the American Rule may arise where litigation produces a common fund for the benefit of a group of claimants, such as produced in a successful class action. The doctrine provides that someone who creates, preserves, or increases the value of a fund in which others have a beneficial interest may obtain reimbursement from the fund for their litigation expenses.

Pursuant to the "common fund" or "equitable fund" approach, attorneys' fees are actually taken directly out of a pool of damages paid by a defendant before the sums are distributed to the successful claimants. The common fund doctrine reflects the equitable restitutionary principle that prevailing parties would otherwise be unjustly enriched if they received the benefits of a lawsuit without sharing in the costs. As such, it is not truly an exception to the American Rule because the fees are not directly shifted to the losing party but are drawn instead from the fund of damages. The plaintiff class shares its recovery with the attorneys in a manner similar to contingency fee arrangements.

(3) Substantial Benefit Theory

Another recognized but rarely used exception to the American Rule is the "substantial benefit" theory. This theory applies only where litigation produces a substantial benefit for a certain class of beneficiaries. In contrast with the common fund exception, the nature of the benefits produced may be intangible rather than leading to creation of a specific fund. One difficulty with imposing attorneys' fees against the benefit recipients, then, is that they do not have a choice in accepting or refusing the benefits conferred. Further, quantifying the benefits of an intangible nature, such as greater corporate accountability or institutional honesty, are inherently difficult to determine.

The requirements for satisfying the substantial benefits doctrine are: (1) the plaintiff must confer a substantial benefit; (2) the class of recipients must be readily identifiable and ascertainable; (3) the benefits must be traceable to the class; and (4) a reasonable basis must exist to ensure that the costs are proportionally spread among the benefitting class. The Supreme Court has characterized the substantial benefit theory as a derivation of the common fund exception, and concluded that the benefit must accrue to the defendant responsible for paying any fees.

(4) Private Attorney General

Another exception to the American Rule provides for fee awards to a successful litigant who acts in a capacity as "private attorney general" with respect to a matter promoting the public interest. The doctrine recognizes that the government necessarily has limited resources to ensure full enforcement of the laws. Therefore, private parties, in limited situations, may fulfill a quasi-governmental role by pursuing litigation to carry out enforcement of laws that reflect strong public policy, such as civil rights or environmental protection. Because the private citizen is benefitting the public good, the rationale is that they should be reimbursed for their litigation costs. Further, often the nature of the remedy obtained in such cases may be injunctive relief, so no fund of damages would exist to offset the expenses incurred. Courts may justify the authority to award fees based upon their inherent equitable powers to carry out the interests of justice.

The private attorney general theory is accepted by numerous states, but it was specifically rejected as a matter of federal common law by the Supreme Court in *Alyeska Pipeline Service Co. v. Wilderness Society* (S.Ct.1975). In *Alyeska,* environmental organizations sought declaratory and injunctive relief that the government's plans for issuance of permits necessary for construction of the Alaskan pipeline violated various federal environmental protection statutes. The plaintiff organizations prevailed, and the Court of Appeals awarded attorneys' fees against the pipeline company based upon theory that they were acting as private attorneys' general. The Supreme Court reversed, reasoning that federal courts should not impose fee awards without express statutory authority. In response to the decision, Congress promptly enacted the Civil Rights Attorney's Fees Awards Act, 42 U.S.C.A. § 1988, to authorize the recovery of attorneys' fees to prevailing parties under a wide variety of civil rights, environmental, and other statutes involving matters of public interest.

Alyeska does not affect the availability of the private attorney general theory under state common law. In *Serrano v. Priest* (Cal.1977) the California Supreme Court held that attorneys' fees could properly be awarded under a state common law theory of private attorney general. The plaintiff had successfully challenged the California public school financing system as being in violation of state constitutional provisions guaranteeing equal protection of the laws. The doctrine was later codified by state statute. Cal. Civ. Proc. Code § 1021.5.

(C) Fee Shifting Statutes

One of the foremost criticisms raised regarding the American Rule has been that a successful claimant would not be made whole where the amount of damages recovered would not offset their litigation expenses. If they only obtained declaratory and injunctive relief, the problem was compounded. Heightened public attention to the issue arose following *Alyeska*, as many expressed concern that the American Rule could undermine the willingness of private parties to pursue legitimate claims in the public interest. In response to these concerns, Congress became active in passing various fee-shifting statutes, particularly with respect to environmental and civil rights. An important illustration is the Civil Rights Attorney's Fees Awards Act of 1976, 42 U.S.C. § 1988, which provides that the court, in its discretion, may allow the prevailing party to recover a reasonable attorneys' fee as part of the costs. Courts presumptively allow recovery of fees to the successful party pursuant to such statutory authorizations and do not require a further showing of bad faith. See Newman v. Piggie Park Enterprises, Inc. (1968).

The federal fee-shifting statutes typically provide for the recovery of attorney fees to the "prevailing party" or "prevailing plaintiff." Considerable litigation has considered the meaning of those terms. The Supreme Court outlined in *Hensley v. Eckerhart* (S.Ct.1983) a basic approach for fee eligibility under The Civil Rights Attorney's Fees Awards Act, 42 U.S.C. § 1988. The Court concluded that a plaintiff is a prevailing party upon succeeding on "any significant issue in litigation which achieves some of the benefit the parties sought in bringing suit."

In *Texas State Teachers Association v. Garland Independent School District* (S.Ct.1989), the Court refined the *Hensley* test for attorney fee awards. The issue in that case was how to interpret "prevailing" when the plaintiff has achieved only partial success on the merits. In *Garland*, several teachers' unions brought constitutional challenges concerning various school board policies limiting union activities and communications. The Court held that fee eligibility was predicated on demonstrating success on a "significant" issue in litigation, but did not require that a plaintiff prevail on the "central" issue in dispute. The Court explained that the principal consideration for fee eligibility is whether the legal relationship of the parties was "materially altered" in a manner consistent with the intentions of Congress in the fee-shifting statute. The degree of overall success relates to the measurement of the fee. Consequently, no fees would be awarded where the plaintiff achieved only technical or *de minimis* success.

The Supreme Court explained these standards further in *Farrar v. Hobby* (S.Ct.1992). The Court held there that a civil rights plaintiff who receives a nominal damages award was a "prevailing party" eligible to receive attorney's fees under 42 U.S.C. § 1988. The Court explained that "a material alteration of the legal relationship occurs [when] the plaintiff becomes entitled to enforce a judgment, consent decree, or settlement against the defendant." This expansive interpretation was curtailed by the Court a few years later in *Buckhannon Board and Care Home, Inc. v. West Virginia Dept. of Health and Human Resources* (S.Ct.2001). In that case, the Court rejected the so-called "catalyst" theory and held that mere voluntary changes in behavior, without securing a court order, did not suffice for a fee award.

Although many federal fee-shifting statutes provide for the recovery of attorney fees to the "prevailing party," many courts have applied a higher standard for awarding fees to successful defendants. In *Christiansburg Garment Co. v. Equal Employment Opportunity Commission* (S.Ct.1978), the Court distinguished between prevailing plaintiffs and prevailing defendants. It held that a prevailing plaintiff in a Title VII discrimination case under the Civil Rights Act of 1964 ordinarily will receive a fee award absent special circumstances, but a prevailing defendant could recover fees only by showing that the plaintiff's claim was "frivolous, unreasonable, or without foundation, even though not brought in subjective bad faith." The Court reasoned that a dual standard for eligibility was justified in order to encourage private attorney general suits to protect civil rights while also to shield such claimants from potential fee liability when the suit was meritorious yet unsuccessful.

(D) Measurement of Fees

The standard approach for calculating attorneys' fees is called the "lodestar" method. The lodestar is calculated by multiplying a reasonable hourly rate for each attorney times the number of hours reasonably spent on the litigation. This amount may be adjusted up or down in light of the "degree of success obtained" in the litigation. *See* Hensley v. Eckerhart (S.Ct.1983). A court may allocate fees for time spent toward successfully litigated specific issues. The claimant must provide an evidentiary basis to justify recovery of fees, and the lack of appropriate documentation may result in reduction or denial of the award. *See* Blanchard v. Bergeron (S.Ct.1989).

The Supreme Court has treated the lodestar figure as presumptively reasonable, subject to adjustment only in rare or exceptional circumstances. Applicants seeking to depart from the lodestar bear a heavy burden to show why an adjustment is necessary. For example, in *City of Burlington v. Dague* (S.Ct.1992) the Court rejected an enhancement of a fee award for the risk of non-recovery under a contingency fee arrangement. The Court found that such an enhancement would likely duplicate factors already reflected in the lodestar calculation.

An award of attorneys' fees under 42 U.S.C. § 1988 does not necessarily need to be proportionate to the amount of damages recovered by the plaintiff in the underlying civil rights action. Rather, the amount of damages is only one of many factors that a court should consider in calculating a reasonable fee under the statute. The Supreme Court noted in *City of Riverside v. Rivera* (S.Ct. 1986) that claims seeking to vindicate civil and constitutional rights may produce relatively small monetary damages yet serve an important public function. A contingent fee limitation would undermine Congressional intent in promoting protection of civil rights by making it harder for individuals to obtain legal representation.

The fee awarded pursuant to § 1988 may differ from amounts owed under a contractual obligation between attorney and client. In *Blanchard v. Bergeron* (S.Ct.1989), the Court held that the fees awarded under the civil rights fee-shifting statute were not automatically governed by or restricted to the amount designated in a contingent fee contract. Although the terms of a contingency fee arrangement were relevant, it did not necessarily dictate what constituted a ''reasonable fee'' under § 1988. For example, in *Venegas v. Mitchell* (S.Ct.1990), an attorney who had successfully represented a client in a civil rights suit sought to recover his contractual contingency fee which significantly exceeded the amount awarded under the fee-shifting statute. The Court upheld the validity of the contractual arrangement, finding that a ''reasonable fee'' under the statute does not override or replace otherwise valid contractual terms. The Court reasoned that

Congress established fee-shifting statutes to benefit the party rather than the lawyer, leaving clients free to bargain on whatever terms they choose to obtain counsel of their choice.

(E) Equal Access to Justice Act

The Equal Access to Justice Act contains provisions for awarding attorneys' fees to private parties who prevail in civil suits against the United States. 28 U.S.C. § 2412. The Act serves as a limited waiver of sovereign immunity and is strictly construed. The purpose of the EAJA is to reduce the disadvantage in economic resources faced by private parties who challenge unreasonable governmental actions.

The Act contains two alternative scenarios for prevailing private parties to recover fees. Under one section, the Act gives the court discretion to impose fees against the federal government to the same extent as private parties pursuant to either common law or statutory authority. 28 U.S.C. § 2412 (b). For example, the court may draw upon equitable principles and impose a fee award where the government acted in bad faith in the conduct of litigation.

Another section authorizes attorney fees to a "prevailing party" unless "the position of the United States was substantially justified or that special circumstances make an award unjust." 28 U.S.C. § 2412(d)(1)(A). The assessment of fees under this provision is mandatory unless "the court finds that the position of the United States was substantially justified or that special circumstances make an award unjust." 28 U.S.C. § 2412(d)(1)(A). Therefore, the Act effectively creates a presumption in favor of a prevailing private party and shifts the burden to the government to demonstrate that its actions were reasonable. The Act specifies that fees must be based upon "prevailing market rates," but places a ceiling of $75 per hour on fees absent a showing of a "special factor" or an adjustment for inflation. 28 U.S.C. § 2412(d)(2)(A)(ii).

(F) Costs Under Federal Rules

Courts also may rely upon Rule 11 under the Federal Rules of Civil Procedure to impose sanctions for abusive litigation practices. The court may assess reasonable attorney fees and expenses incurred against a party responsible for vexatious or frivolous litigation. The rule may be implicated where pleadings or motions lack a sufficient factual or legal basis or are filed for improper reasons. One function of the rule is to shift the costs of litigation and compensate a party for expenses directly resulting from abusive practices. The rule is also educational and rehabilitative in that it allows the court to use monetary sanctions to punish and deter attorneys responsible for violating the federal rules.

Several other statutory and procedural provisions are available to a court to deter litigation abuse. For example, 28 U.S.C. § 1927 permits a court to assess litigation costs against an attorney who "multiplies the proceedings" in a case "unreasonably and vexatiously." Fed.R.Civ.P. 37 permits sanctions against parties or persons who unjustifiably resist discovery. Appellate courts, pursuant to Fed.R.App.P. 38, may impose cost sanctions against an appellant for bringing a frivolous appeal.

Chapter 20

DECLARATORY REMEDIES

(A) Nominal Damages

The relationship between substantive rights and remedies has been a theme throughout this Nutshell. Because a right is only as great as the remedy that vindicates it, the variety of remedies available for particular rights contributes to their importance. Moreover, if there is no remedy for a right, then the right is a "paper tiger" without means of enforcement.

An award of nominal damages is not an insignificant remedy in this context, even though it provides no monetary recovery to the plaintiff other than a token amount. Its significance is that the award serves as a declaration of the plaintiff's victory on the substantive claim. That remedy is a limited one, but not an entirely empty one.

A court awards nominal damages when a plaintiff has been able to establish the violation of a right but cannot establish the requirements of remedies that would otherwise be available. It may be used in a trespass case, for example, when the owner of the land cannot prove any loss from the defendant's invasion. The function of nominal damages in such a case is to ascertain the rights of the parties and thus to deter future invasion of the land.

Nominal damages also serve an important role in civil rights litigation. In *Carey v. Piphus* (S.Ct. 1978) the Supreme Court declined to endorse presumed damages for violations of due process rights, but did permit nominal damages in cases where no loss is established. The significance of the nominal damages is that it can support an award of attorneys' fees under The Civil Rights Attorney's Fees Awards Act of 1976. Without such an incentive to vindicate civil rights, it would be difficult for most plaintiffs to pursue a claim. The other significance of a nominal damages award is that many jurisdictions permit punitive damages under appropriate circumstances, even when the damages award is just nominal.

(B) Declaratory Judgments

The declaratory judgment is a statutory remedy available under modern state and federal law. It gives courts the power to determine the rights or legal relations of parties to a justiciable controversy. This statutory remedy was developed in response to a gap in the common law that no specific means existed to declare the status or rights of parties to resolve certain types of disputes. Apart from several specialized declaratory remedies, such as bills to quiet title or cancellation of instruments, the closest counterpart under common law was nominal damages. Those remedies were much more limited in scope and application than subsequent declaratory judgment statutory schemes.

The statutory authorization for declaratory relief does not create new rights nor confer or expand the subject matter jurisdiction of courts, however, but requires an independent basis for the court to assert jurisdiction. The Federal Declaratory Judgment Act, codified at 28 U.S.C. §§ 2201, 2202, has been characterized as an "enabling" Act which confers a discretion on courts rather than an absolute right upon litigants. *See* Public Service Commission of Utah v. Wycoff Company (S.Ct.1952). The orders are reviewable as final judgments and have *res judicata* effect.

Constitutional and prudential considerations also affect the power and propriety of federal courts to issue declaratory judgments. The federal statute requires that a case or controversy exist in order to satisfy constitutional standards for the exercise of judicial power. *See* Aetna Life Insurance Co. v. Haworth (S.Ct.1937). The dispute must involve genuinely conflicting claims rather than a hypothetical concern or an advisory opinion. Courts also retain considerable discretion with respect to issuance of declaratory judgments, and may refuse to render a decree if it would not terminate the controversy or serve a useful purpose.

A declaratory judgment is unique among remedies in that it does not provide compensation nor mandate or prohibit specific actions. In contrast with equitable decrees such as injunctions, it is not considered an extraordinary remedy and therefore does not require a showing that other remedies are inadequate. A declaration of rights does not coerce or bind parties *in personam*. Once rights are established, however, a declaratory judgment will pragmatically influence parties to tailor their subsequent actions to correspond to the decree.

A declaratory judgment may be the only order issued by a court, or it can be used in combination with others. For example, if a landowner plans to erect a fence and an adjoining neighbor disputes the location of the boundary line, a declaratory judgment can resolve the controversy over the property rights. If the construction of the fence is imminent, the court may also issue a prohibitory injunction to prevent its installation. In the exercise of its discretion, the court may stay its hand in issuing a declaratory judgment unless all property owners potentially affected by the decree were parties to the suit.

A common reason that claimants seek declaratory judgments is to ascertain their rights or status, such as under a contract or coverage of a statute, prior to incurring a breach or violation. Because courts do not render advisory opinions, however, a concrete dispute must already exist in order to justify the court's action. Further, if the breach or violation has already occurred, a court may decide that a declaratory order would not serve a useful purpose and decline to exercise its discretion.

Declaratory relief with respect to defining statutory coverage has been used in various civil and criminal contexts, such as determining the scope of penal, taxation, and licensing statutes on the state and federal level. Although the declaratory judgment does not order a party to comply directly with the statute, it has an indirectly coercive effect by setting forth the statutory requirements and effectively giving notice that non-compliance risks violation of the law.

A court also may decline to issue declaratory relief if its timeliness has already passed. For example, if criminal proceedings have already been initiated, a court will likely refuse to order a declaratory judgment regarding the scope of the applicable penal statute. In refusing to exercise jurisdiction, the court may appropriately cite reasons of judicial economy, respect for the ongoing proceedings, and recognition that the claimant may raise the same issues of statutory coverage as a defense in the criminal trial.

The Declaratory Judgment Act confers broad discretion on federal courts regarding the propriety of exercising jurisdiction. In *Wilton v. Seven Falls Co.* (S.Ct.1995) the Supreme Court described this discretion: "Congress sought to place a remedial arrow in the district court's quiver; it created an opportunity, rather than a duty, to grant a new form of relief to qualifying litigants."

Strong considerations of federalism, comity, and judicial economy affect the exercise of discretion by a federal court in situations where a pending state court proceeding involves matters related to a federal suit. A federal court may abstain from exercising jurisdiction in order to allow a state court to decide important matters of state law. The Supreme Court also applied abstention doctrine to prevent a federal court from interfering with complex matters involving state administrative processes and potentially disrupt important state policy. *See* Railroad Comm'n of Texas v. Pullman (S.Ct.1941). Similarly, *Brillhart v. Excess Ins. Co.* (S.Ct.1942) and its progeny provide guidance for the exercise of discretion when concurrent state proceedings are pending. In addition to basic principles of comity and federalism, other factors may influence the decision of a federal court to issue a declaratory judgment where state proceedings are pending. They include: discouragement of forum shopping, convenience of parties and witnesses, effectiveness of alternative remedies, and judicial economy in avoiding duplicative or piecemeal litigation.

*

INDEX

References are to Pages

MISTAKE—Cont'd
Reformation, 200
Restitution, 200
Unilateral, 201

MITIGATION OF DAMAGES
    See Avoidable Consequences

MONEY HAD AND RECEIVED
    See Assumpsit

MUTUALITY OF REMEDY
Employment contract, 41
Limitation and abolition, 42–43
Mutuality of obligation distinguished, 42
Negative version, 41
Specific performance, requirement in, 40–43

NOMINAL DAMAGES
    Generally, 246–247
Actual injury, not required, 246
Attorneys' fees, sufficiency, 239–240
Constitutional violation, 247
Declaratory judgments, compared, 247
Procedural due process, denial, 247
Punitive damages, relation, 191

NORRIS-LAGUARDIA ACT
Anti-injunction provisions, 20–21
Contempt related to, 84–85

NUISANCE
Adequacy of legal remedy, injunction, 2, 102–107
Anticipatory, probability of harm, 105
Anti-injunction acts, 105
Balancing of equities, generally, 102
Boomer v. Atlantic Cement, 31–32
Coming to the nuisance, 106
Damages, generally, 103
Defined, 102
Economic loss, 103
Factories, 31–32, 103–104
Feedlot, 106–107
Gambling operation, 109
Half-way house, 106
Injunction against, 102–107
Public interest, 31–32, 104–107

QUANTUM MERUIT
   See Assumpsit; Restitution

QUASI-CONTRACT
   See Assumpsit; Restitution

REFORMATION
Defined, 136
Mistake, 136
Rescission compared, 136

RESCISSION
   See Restitution

RESTITUTION
   Generally, 7–8, 199
Assumpsit, history, 209–211
Benefit, generally, 199
Commingling of funds, 218–221
Common Counts, 204–205
Constructive trusts, 205–209
Contract breach, generally, 112–114
Damages, compared, 8
Defenses
   Bona fide purchaser, 221–225
   Change of position, 225–227
   Tracing, 216–221
   Volunteers, 212–216
Equitable lien, 205–209
Fraud, 202–203
History, 210
Implied in law contract, 203–205
Improvements to land, 207–209
Measurement, 199, 202–211
Misrepresentation, 202–203
Mistake, 200–202
Priority over other creditors, 206
Quantum meruit, 203–205
Quasi-contract, history, 206, 211–212
Reformation, 201
Rescission, 201
Specific restitution, 206
Tracing, 216–221
Unjust enrichment, generally, 199
Waiver of tort, 209–211

†